Cloud Computing...
Commoditizing IT

The Imperative Venture For Every Enterprise

By

Rod Kamal Ghani Agha, Ph.D.

authorHOUSE®

AuthorHouse™
1663 Liberty Drive
Bloomington, IN 47403
www.authorhouse.com
Phone: 1 (800) 839-8640

Published by AuthorHouse 06/11/2015

ISBN: 978-1-5049-0504-6 (sc)
ISBN: 978-1-5049-0503-9 (hc)
ISBN: 978-1-5049-0505-3 (e)

Library of Congress Control Number: 2015909001

Contents

Dedication

I dedicate this book to the memory of my mother in-law Hana Alnaqib. Proceeds of this book will be donated to cancer research.

Acknowledgements

Above all, I want to thank my wife Zana and my two sons, Leith and Zade, for their endless support in spite of all the time it took me away from them. It was a long and difficult journey for them.

Thank you, Mom and Dad, and my brothers for putting up with me.

Anything is possible if you want it bad enough.

Love you all with all my heart
Rod Kamal Ghani Agha

Who should read this book?

This book is aimed at information technology (IT) professionals at all levels including CIOs, CTOs, IT directors, managers, and engineers thinking about cloud computing, IT transformation, and how it may impact their organization. Also, this is a book for IT graduate students, both MBA and doctoral, who seek to learn a great deal about emerging technologies and formal research methods theories. This book can benefit IT management consulting firms as well, to help their clients who are thinking or implementing cloud computing as a key initiative in their organization.

This book we discuss how cloud computing is commoditizing IT, and is cloud computing a real threat or irresistible opportunity? How cloud computing is revolutionizing the financial industry and the way we conduct business.

Part I we explain how to build a successful cloud computing strategy, also share details of the survey results we conducted in my Ph.D. dissertation on cloud computing adoption models and the decision-making variables and factors that take place.

Part II of the book is ideal for graduate students and doctoral candidates who are working on empirical academic research. We discuss the cloud computing adoption life cycle, theory of innovation diffusion, research questions, hypotheses, measurement instruments, the way that emotions drive technology adoption, and dependent and independent variables.

Part III of the book includes relevant case study samples, beneficial for those who are looking for writing in an academic style and case study research.

Rod Ghani Agha Ph.D.
Scottsdale, Arizona
February, 2015

Introduction

Cloud computing is a relatively new IT metaphor, relating to a group of remote servers and software applications that can be accessed on demand via self-service portals, by users of the internet. Cloud technology is rapidly becoming ubiquitous in every industry and, in fact, in every aspect of technology usage.

Organizations that are willing to adjust in order to deal with this change will be able to survive the next wave of technology transformation. More than ever, organizations must become flexible and collaborative, both internally and externally, to deliver continuous IT services on demand. Cloud computing aims to enable the entire business ecosystem by simplifying service offerings to meet customer needs. Those who don't adapt quickly are more likely to suffer and, ultimately may be unable to survive.

IT is Undergoing a Metamorphosis Period

Much like butterflies and moths that pass through stages of transformation in their life cycles, IT is going through a similar transformation period. The only way for organizations to survive is to embrace and experience this transformation in all its stages. The world is changing to a shared economy and collaborative consumption, as evidenced by Uber and Airbnb, enabling peer groups to act as one enormous service delivery entity. We want to watch the movie but not own the DVD. We like to read the book not having to purchase the book.

Organizations are leveraging the cloud to cut costs and deliver better customer experience, rapidly and consistently. Cloud computing has created a new ecosystem that is controlled by end points to deliver and receive services. Organizations who embrace this new ecosystem, adopting cloud computing and the mindsets it personifies, have guaranteed their existence where others have folded. Think about what Amazon has done to the bookstores, Netflix to Blockbuster Video, Online news Yahoo and Google to the newspaper and magazine industries. These familiar names have dramatically disrupted the market ecosystem, driving iconic names into obscurity and changing the very models by which we do business.

> **In 1961, Stanford professor John McCarthy was one of the first to suggest a time-share, service bureau computing model.**

Cloud computing commoditizing IT

Cloud computing has re-categorized the value of business, transforming the values of commodities to service experience. For example flour is a commodity which is priced lower than a packaged product, backed bread is priced higher than flour, and the bread when served in the restaurant setting is priced higher than the bread would otherwise be. As you go through the value chain, the revenue increases as well as the perceived experience by the customer. The top of the hierarchy is a higher customization of the experience, which means higher business transformation.

Cloud computing services are increasingly engaging the consumer to a better experience and higher value proposition by on-demand, instantaneous, consistent delivery model with greater ease of use. The key element of cloud computing is creating a higher value and better customer experience than the basic product being consumed.

> In A 1996 paper, The Self-governing Internet: Coordination by Design, MIT researchers used the term "cloud" to describe foundational elements of today's movement.

Is Cloud Computing a Strategic advantage?

Most IT decision makers surveyed believe at this time cloud is a strategic and necessary initiative in order to protect their market share and to enhance their competitive advantage. However, what still remains unknown is how much of an impact is cloud creating? What's the ROI? Will it grow only market share without profit? Will the additional productivity actually reduce cost and help the bottom-line? By how much? Is cloud computing about survival or is it in pursuit of better value? These are key questions we will be discussing later in the book.

In order to get the answer we must understand the difference between the terms correlated and causal, to clarify the relationship between profitability and commutative success and the investment in cloud computing.

For example, we may hypothesize that ice-cream causes drowning. Let's look at the relationship. More people eat ice-cream in the summer. More people go swimming in the summer. Also, more drowning accidents happen in the summer, at the same time people are swimming and eating ice-cream. So it happens that there is a correlation between eating ice-cream and drowning, but ice-cream is obviously not the cause of drowning.

Let's take another example, that high cholesterol causes heart attacks. In this case however, it has proven medically that high cholesterol causes heart attacks, making this a causal relationship rather than a correlational one.

Buying new running shoes will not help you lose weight once you wear them; it will take hard work and dedication and you also must still control your diet and eat less in order to really show results. Simply investing in the cloud may not reap the value the organization is expecting. There are many other factors that could enhance or degrade the value proposition, directly or indirectly.

We need to know, if we invest and build the cloud, whether the results will directly impact the organization profitability and help the organizations competitive edge and whether the investment is causal. How will it help my organization sell more and increase profitability?

How do we know that investment in cloud is the root cause of the higher profit and not the result of another function? It's difficult to declare with 100% certainty that the cause of increased profitability and competitive success is only due to the investment in cloud computing. There could be other variables that are outside of this relationship that help the result to conclude as such.

If we believe cloud computing is a game changer, then we must consider the realization of not adopting the cloud can be fatal to future of the organization. As the popularity of cloud grows and cloud adoption increases, the strategic importance decreases. Much like any utility, certainly in today's world an IT company can't claim its competitive advantage because they have utilities such as water or electricity. All the competitors have those as well, therefore the utility advantage has lost its strategic advantage.

Cloud computing is no different, and this may be the time to leverage cloud and win a strategic advantage, at least until the competition leverages cloud as well and the field again becomes competitive. However you don't ever want to be left behind because that can mean loss of business or even the livelihood of the business.

> **In September 2009, Amazon EC2 launched more than 50,000 virtual machine instances in a 24-hour period within a single region.**

Cloud Computing a Real Threat, Irresistible Opportunity

Cloud computing is the essence of this ecosystem disruption, transforming startup names into giants with immense wealth and driving once-iconic names into bankruptcy. Cloud computing, for a variety of companies, is a strategic need for their competitive advantage, essential to their existence. Others will blame the cloud for their failure to compete and their demise. Cloud computing is disrupting every dimension of every business model.

Cloud computing allows you to harness every speck of resource, regardless of the geographic location. Cloud computing will enhance the utilization of servers and expands the application beyond the IT organization. Cloud computing provides ubiquitous access and location independence.

The new IT is delivering IT as a service and may be by an external organization called IT cloud provider. The new IT is silo-shattering in that it integrates IT operations and applications into one unit to deliver rapid value to the customer from undisclosed locations. Cloud computing is virtual and dynamically scalable, accessible anytime, anywhere, using any device, hence the term on-demand availability. The unique characteristics about cloud computing are its elasticity, available capacity ready to be consumed on demand.

When consumers access applications online, they are abstracted from the IT infrastructure environment. Consumers pay only for what they consume; consequently, it's also called a utility model, much like the electric and water utility companies.

> **In late 2009 the city of Los Angeles reported that it will likely save $5 million by switching from Novell's GroupWise desktop software to cloud-based Google Apps.**

Cloud computing is irresistible, an attractive business model promising huge savings. Therefore, cloud computing has become the single most important strategic initiative for most organizations. Companies whom are adopting cloud computing as an enabler for their business, leveraging external infrastructure at a lower cost, providing more services that will give them a better competitive advantage.

However, many issues such as security risks, loss of control over the data, identity theft, vendor lock in, vendor instability, application instability, complex integration with existing systems, unclear vendor charges and inconsistent savings values, have caused poor consumer experience which have slowed down the adoption rate of cloud computing.

Outsource vs. Insource

Most organizations do use external cloud computing (SaaS) for non-critical functions or non-customer impacting, often called inward and not outward facing services. Today most IT organizations are challenged with creating their own private cloud, compelled to build a strong redundant Infrastructure foundation and change business processes to meet the new business rules. IT must automate and orchestrate the deployment of the resources and it must be metered so it can be measured for charge back to show the value provided and to keep track of capacity.

Hybrid IT

Unlike the traditional IT delivery model, cloud computing is an on-demand model, therefore the request must be instantly deployed once the request is submitted by the consumer. This is a radical shift from the way IT operates today, not to mention the capital investment that must be committed by the organization as a leap of faith. Hence, many IT organizations are leaning towards a brokerage model by purchasing cloud resources and reselling it to the consumer.

The hybrid IT approach seems to be a safer bet for organizations looking to experiment with cloud computing and drive the value without taking a huge risk. Hybrid IT can enable your consumer to leverage the agility (on demand delivery) of cloud without having to commit to a huge capital outlay.

Even with hybrid IT, there are still technical challenges with significate integration points internally and externally. Security risks remain a factor in the decision maker's mind, a barrier to entry that influences the cultural shift of fear and trust issues. Thus, cloud computing is a serious threat to the organization's existence but also an irresistible opportunity.

IT organizations who adopt cloud computing will position their organization to thrive in much more volatile markets and will drive business to compete in their own segment. Those who can build a better service delivery model will end up defeating their competition.

The future of IT organizations will be a virtual data center delivering metered self-services directly to the users. Moving to a utility base model, or variable cost operating model, seems to be more efficient economically, since the organization pays only for what's being used. As user consumes services, such as servers, disk storage and software applications, they are only paying for what they use.

Servers can be provisioned, built, in minutes without human intervention. Physical servers are virtualized and made available as resources, they are then pooled and offered as resources to multi-tenant users. Controlled by an automated capacity management, also referred to as resource elasticity, is one of the main characteristics of cloud computing. As the demand increases, the resource pool can extend and reach for more capacity. Resources are assigned a utilization calendar to be returned to the resource pool when the time of the request expires. Users are only charged for consumption of that particular resource and time used.

Today, most organizations spend about 6% of their revenue on IT operations. IT spends about 80% of its budget on maintenance, licensing, and staffing. Cloud computing offers a shared, multi-tenancy utility model that will shift operation expenses where the user pays only for what's used. Cloud computing transforms information technology to a utility service provider and not a product supplier. Business units depend on IT service providers which are often outsourced to a third party, much like the public power grid supplying electricity.

The traditional IT organization hierarchy pyramid as we know it coming to an end. The new IT model gives the business unit a high degree of autonomy. Services will be available as they are needed and delivered instantly, in many cases without getting IT involved. The traditional IT will be transformed to a service support model, managing capacity and offering more services via electronic order portal referred to as the service catalog. The new delivery mechanism of information for all enterprises and end users have no time, location or device boundaries.

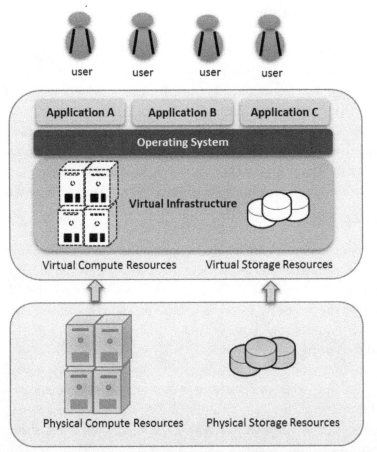

Cloud computing by Stack © Rod Ghani 2015

However, cloud computing systems and software standards are not fully defined, leaving many companies to define their own standards, causing interoperability and data synchronization issues. Therefore many organizations are challenged with picking the best approach to cloud adoption.

> Yankee Group recently reported that 75% of enterprises say they are earmarking no more than a third of their 2010 IT budgets to the cloud.

The New IT Must Compete For Business

Cloud computing cuts through all layers of businesses and IT hierarchy, creating a disruptive model to business processes and IT service delivery. Cloud computing is transforms IT organizations which causes a fundamental shift to the IT delivery model.

Cloud computing commoditizing IT organizations and are no longer monopolizing the business. It has become evident that IT leaders must compete with cloud providers in order to earn the business of their own organization.

Innovative cloud providers are taking advantage of the organization's vulnerability by offering new IT services that can be delivered rapidly, at a lesser cost and based on a consumption model, leaving the IT organization on the defensive. IT organizations that don't take advantage of the cloud computing revolution may become irrelevant and maybe be replaced by a third party provider.

CIOs are still trying to figure out how to harness the highest value of cloud computing with the least amount of risk and disruption to the IT environment. Our research found that CIOs are concerned about performance, availability, security, and systems stability. Many are still trying to figure out how to implement cloud strategy, take advantage of the cost reduction and rapid delivery for a better consumer experience.

Current IT organizations have a limited leverage with software vendors due to their enterprise licensing model. The traditional enterprise software model is disproportionate to its full utilization, meaning, most organizations use a limited functionally and time of the application, yet they pay for the full cost of the license, inefficient and costly model. Hence the cloud computing utility model, because pay per consumption becomes more appealing financially. In addition cloud computing offers elasticity and immediate systems availability without worrying about licensing, and capacity running out. This is yet another value proposition to the adoption of cloud computing.

In addition, cloud computing can reduce operational cost. It offers a higher service level, upsizing and downsizing systems resources, automating IT services and processes, delivering consistent service levels rapidly and delivering IT as a Service.

IT automation is the glue that seals the disparate, manual, non sequential functions and make them look as one unit delivering cloud computing. Yet, some organizations fear IT automation, mistakenly believing that automation may lead to a replacement of human resources with automated machine processes to reduce labor. Generally this is not an accurate assumption. IT automation aims to increase productivity and quality beyond what is possible with the current IT team. IT automation will deliver services consistently that can be scaled to higher quality levels. When automation is achieved, the IT staff become more effective and efficient, and able to manage more processes than before.

Is Cloud a competitive advantage for the organization?

Most certainly yes. IT transforms commodities such as computers, ram, and storage into service for a better customer experience, much like a restaurant prepares a meal from commodity products. The quality and the level of service will determine if the customer is willing to return or will choose instead to go to another competitor.

Organizations can significantly differentiate themselves by adopting cloud computing, gaining a huge competitive advantage until their competitors do the same.

> **IT can be a differentiator that allows the organization to gain a competitive strategic advantage until their competitors do the same.**

Cloud computing has transformed the actual delivery model from being a single IT organization building product for the business to building a partnership to co-develop the services with the actual consumers and external providers. This type of transformation creates unity and partnerships among the business units, external vendors and IT organizations. All parties can share the value and the experience of the cloud and the risks that come with it. It shifts the focus from IT providing only tools to building a true competitive business advantage with the customers.

In many ways cloud computing has democratized IT, much like the internet democratized the news TV networks and GPS democratized atlas maps.

Cloud computing unleashes and accelerates the innovation cycle by dimensioning the constraints of the traditional IT model, transforming it to co-strategies between the business units and IT organization for continuous improvement and to be continuously perfected. Overall, achieving competitive success doesn't come from one thing but from many small things done well.

Cloud computing frees the organization from the worries of operations and lets it focus of business differentiators for competitive advantage, much like retailers focusing on designs and product positioning while they outsource distribution and logistics.

The Utilitization of IT

I'm tokening the term *Utilitization,* which is transforming IT to a utility service, or running IT as a utility model. On demand, anytime, anywhere, metered service, wherein users only pay for usage.

Cloud computing maybe referred to as the utilitization of IT, much like the water, electric and cable utilities. Within this paradigm, IT can be provided by cloud providers and in some cases traditional IT can be reduced drastically, allowing the organization to focus on delivering a competitive strategic advantage to meet their business objectives more quickly.

To achieve the competitive advantage is to adopt and innovate more quickly than the competitors.

Cloud computing runs on ubiquitous networks and systems that provides an inherited advantage to the customer's intimacy and personalization experience. In order to win the competitive advantage, cloud services must be a game changer, differentiating and unlike other services in the market.

For example, the iPad comes with a differentiating advantage, i.e., the App store. Likewise, Tesla is not just another car with a different style; it's a game changer: a car that runs on battery. With cloud computing, the service provider has the ability to capture the consumer's behaviors and collect seamlessly their buying and service behavior. These purchasing behaviors can be used to your advantage to continue to capture their interests and their purchasing habits. The more you know about the consumer, the more your organization can translate these behaviors to drive higher revenue, big data and elastic searching are two common terms are used to identify user behavior. It's like new money found. This is why we believe cloud computing is a strategic advantage with a unique ability to help increase revenue.

Cloud computing brings the business and its IT function far closer from the traditional IT model. It is imperative for IT and the business itself to interpret the service buying habits and turn them in to a better consumer experience for the future. The consumer experience can be categorized as high value, low cost, ease of use, consistently meets or exceeds expectations and reliable.

> **Research and Markets analysts are more bullish, expecting cloud computing to be a $160.2 billion market by 2015.**

Another characteristic of cloud computing is cloud computing democratizes and accelerates the innovation cycle, which increase the number of trials. This lowers the cost of failure and hence encourages more innovative, uncertain, risky, and creative ideas. Cloud computing lowers infrastructure and software licenses costs, therefore IT is commoditized enabling not only IT but business units to experiment and innovate to strike a higher competitive advantage. This in turn enhances the customer experience, building a better brand and achieving a greater level of global recognition.

> Tony Scott, "Even technology that's a commodity still provides business flexibility." –Tony Scott, CTO General Motors...

Network Organization

No matter which successful, recognizable manufacturing organization we look into, we will find the brand is more of a name that's carrying the customer experience. The actual organization is focused on being a differentiator with items such as product design and new innovations, while the majority of the parts (if not all the parts) are manufactured by hundreds (or thousands) of suppliers and partners. That is a phenomenon known as network organization.

For example, General Motors, focus is on delivering better products and more features, while their hundreds of suppliers are executing and building the parts to be assembled. Draw the same parallel when it comes to cloud computing. It's not about IT doing all the work anymore; it's about IT controlling the partners to deliver the highest value and achieve the best customer experience at the lowest cost.

Cloud computing has turned IT and business ecosystems into cloud network organizations that must rapidly and swiftly adopt to changes, especially when there is a complex business model and a high rate of change in place.

Network organizations must be careful in choosing the cloud provider's partnership when adopting cloud strategy, because essentially we are redefining the boundaries of the organization. The lines between the customer, the business, and IT are blurred without a clear line of demarcation and, therefore, it would have a direct impact on the internal business policies, physical, virtual and human structure of the organization.

Cloud computing is orchestrated by fragmented collaboration to provide reliable consistent services, created by diverse but complementing disciplines to deliver an intimate, reliable consumer experience.

> **Data and content related uses are the next big drivers according to IDC, including back-up, distribution and storage.**

Rod Kamal Ghani Agha, Ph.D.

Cloud Computing Framework

Cloud computing has forced business to enter a new era of economic model, to transform the business to deliver intimate customer collaboration, and to challenge the business to be a differentiator in the market, leveraging IT services, breaking the formal hierarchy, and

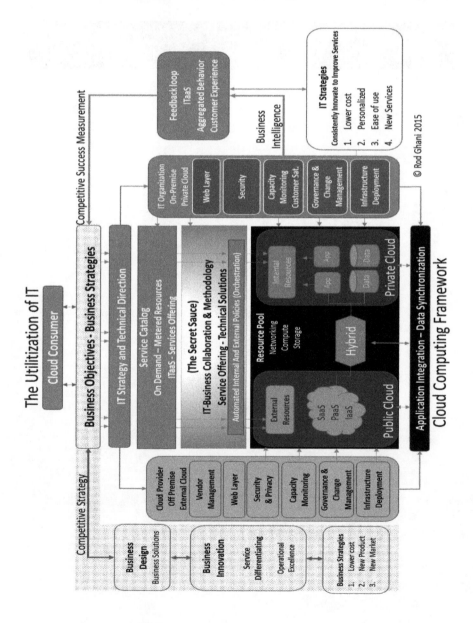

classic protocols. Cloud computing is about transforming the traditional IT product delivery to a utility model that's available on demand at a lower cost and a higher value. Cloud computing turns IT and the business into one unit working on a single business strategy and business objective. The business will continuously evaluate customer's behavior and buying habits to realign its competitive strategy to achieve a higher value.

As for IT, it must adopt its technical direction and IT strategy based on the business strategic direction. IT must evaluate its direction based on the business needs, the service offering, the most effective methodology to achieve the least cost, and the most and best reliable systems performance. IT must choose providing services on-premises, off premises (outsourced), or a combination of both in a hybrid cloud. These decisions will be based on cost, most fit partnership, available APIs, integration points, security and privacy risks, and compliance. IT will continue to manage external and internal relationships and provide continuous feedback, leveraging the aggregated data on customer behavior, volume, the history of services. This feedback is invaluable for the business, and it is seamless, without having to bother the customer.

> "If we've learned one thing from the 1990s, it's that big bang IT-driven initiates rarely produce expected returns." There is no consistent correlation between IT spending and corporate performance.
> Steven Alter, a professor at the University of California, San Francisco, argued that "IT Doesn't Matter' convey a fallacy."

Cloud Computing Services

1. Software as a Service (SaaS)

Consumers use software application over the internet as a service on demand. Such applications are accessed from a web browser, while the software and data are stored in the cloud.

Is most likely the main driver for the cloud computing adoption, making the application available for consumption to the user. Unlike the traditional licensing model, the user pays only when using the application.

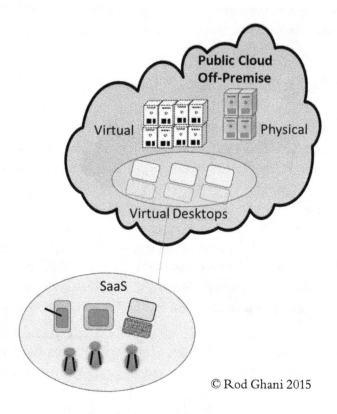

© Rod Ghani 2015

SaaS software vendors may host the application on their own web servers or they may rent IaaS and/or PaaS from others. Examples of SaaS vendors are salesforce.com, Facebook, Microsoft office 365, Google email and apps.

2. Platform as a Service (PaaS)

Virtualizing the platform tools and creating the development environment for developers to consume on demand via service portals.

PaaS provides a platform for the applications to run as a service, securely and reliably. Depending on the business case, compliance and technical requirements, your IT organization may choose to run your application using an on-premises internal private cloud or broker the service and leverage an external PaaS provider to run the origination's applications and outsource the platform.

3. Infrastructure as a Service (IaaS)

This is the foundation and first layer of cloud computing stack, essentially converting all physical infrastructure to virtual infrastructures such as servers and network equipment made available as resources for rent.

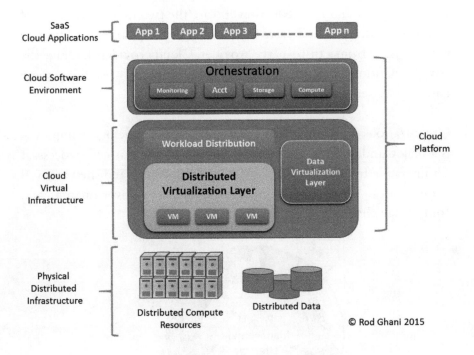

Infrastructure is facilities, electricity, networking equipment like routers and switches, computers, RAM, storage, and other hardware that is virtualized to run OS and databases and applications as a service. Rather than purchasing servers and build data centers, your IT organization can choose to run your applications on- premises (private cloud) or rent the infrastructure and the equipment to run your applications. The service is typically billed on a utility computing basis and the amount of resources consumed (and therefore the cost) will typically reflect the level of activity. It is an evolution of web hosting and virtual private server offerings.

> **A late 2009 survey by Taneja Group found that 92% of Test/Dev operations are using shared infrastructures, or "private" clouds.**

The Disruption of Cloud Computing Adoption

Business agility and cost reduction and are the two main advantages of cloud computing. Cloud users can reduce their capital expenditure by renting usage from a third-party provider. Cloud providers leverage the cost distribution by sharing the cost of the Infrastructure among many customers often called tenants or hoteling model.

Organizations must understand that the adoption of cloud computing is a major undertaking and quite disruptive to the business process. It is imperative to consider the impact on the business and the technical complexities, integration points, data security, governmental and compliance challenges.

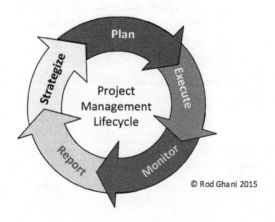

© Rod Ghani 2015

Feasibility studies must be conducted to forecast the performance and the stability of enterprise applications, and the likelihood to be cloud enabled. A disciplined, proven methodology is critical to gain an accurate assessment of the required effort, investment, and the value proposition.

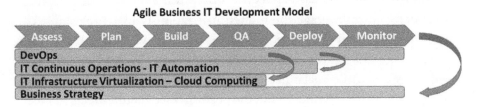

The organization must have a clear business objective with established, measurable goals to be achieved. Is the objective to reduce operational cost, or is it about reducing capital budget? Is the objective about delivering services quicker, more consistently, for a better customer experience?

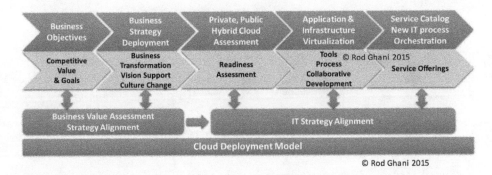

© Rod Ghani 2015

Virtualizing the Data Center

The first ingredient necessary to transition to cloud computing is the virtualization of the IT infrastructure. Operations must carefully look to strategic capacity plans that will expand and contract to accurately forecast user demand to maximize usage of the physical hardware and gain the most efficiencies.

This is a complicated and complex process, IT staff must understand the physical and virtual density and the applications' behavior in the virtual environment. Performance measure and load testing will be critical to the end result user experience. Applying resource policies and building the orchestration is the next hurdle that IT staff must overcome. Striking the right balance between resource availability and anticipating users demand to leverage the highest utilization is an art that must be carefully deployed. Deployed resources (vCPU, vRAM, vDisk, OS, applications) must have expiration dates to return to the resource pool and be ready to be reclaimed. IT staff must understand the business objectives clearly and understand the performance requirements to meet the user expectations.

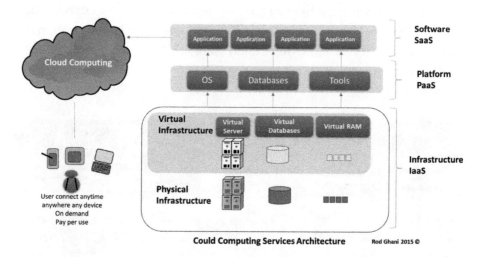

Could Computing Services Architecture   Rod Ghani 2015 ©

Cloud services runs over virtualized hardware and software resources are provisioned and orchestrated dynamically. These services run on redundant resources and can adjust their capacity for more resources as the demand increases automatically.

Cloud computing architecture is based on a reliable virtual infrastructure, platform, and software which can be owned by the organization or rented from a 3rd party cloud provider. Cloud services are delivered via the internet over servers with different levels of virtualization technologies from data centers. Consumers can access these services on demand from anywhere, anytime, from any device, and only pay for the usage of the service.

As more IT organizations transform their IT functions to external services, there will be an excess of unused capacity in their IT infrastructure. IT organizations should leverage these capacities to build more resilient services as well as lowering software and maintenance costs.

As the cloud adaption gains popularity, business units will replace traditional IT with a third party IaaS provider, gaining freedom and changing relationship between IT and the business organization. IT operations must focus more on business process and managed services, while IT staff will shift their role from component product to process management and governance. IT will transition from physical infrastructure on-premises to virtual farms that can be hosted on- or off-premise.

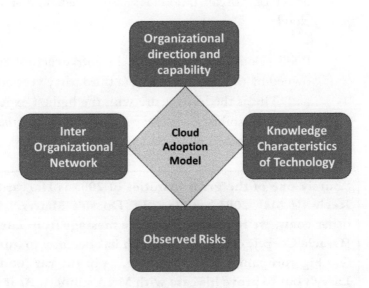

Source: Rod Ghani doctorate research of cloud adoption 2014

"Average outage on cloud services is 7.5 hours per year, giving the cloud an availability rate of 99.9%

Types of Cloud deployments

Cloud computing can be deployed under different models, these models are:

1- Private cloud – on-premise cloud that's built inside the organization's firewalls.
   a. This is the most secure cloud model.
   b. The infrastructure, platform and applications are owned by the IT organization.
   c. This model is mostly used for core business applications that are unique and specific to the organization. Most organizations leverage the private cloud model to provision systems on demand for their development and testing environment.

2- Community Cloud - a private cloud used by a community under one organization. It's also called multi-tenant private cloud.

3- Public cloud – Off- premise IT infrastructure and platform owned by the cloud provider (a third party vendor).
   a. This is the least secure with the highest exposure in risk and stability *model, since it's hosted by an external vendor.*
   b. Most commom model for non-critical applications.

> **"Surely one of the great inanities of 2003 is Harvard Business Review's May 2003 article, "IT Doesn't Matter." From the other coast, we're getting the same message from Larry Ellison [Oracle Corp.], claiming that tech has become mature--only a few big companies will dominate, as in the car industry. And Larry's out to prove his case with M&A silliness. As it turns out, Larry and HBR are half right, and therefore totally wrong."**
> **-George F. Colony, CEO and President, Forrester Research**

4- Hybrid cloud – The cloud infrastructure and platform is a combination of internal and external integration that works as one cloud. This model gives the organization the control over the data being hosted locally and still leverage external resources and services.

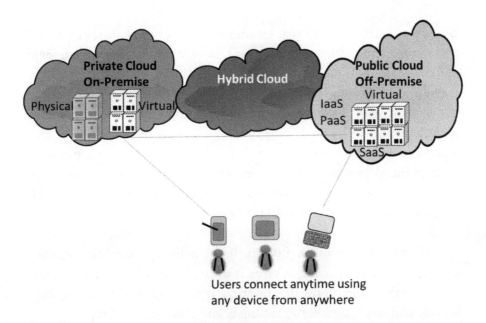

Users connect anytime using any device from anywhere

PART I

Building Cloud Strategy

Executive Overview

By now we have learned that businesses must leverage innovation and emerging technologies to stay relevant, in order to continue to compete and maintain their market share. The proposition of going to the cloud is tempting, offering low entry cost, and rental models make it easy to experiment with. Often however the adoption fails for many reasons including unclear business objectives or the lack of commitment and direction. Cloud is viewed as a disruptive IT process, accompanied with political pressures and job security uncertainty. Cloud is about delivering IT as a service, and this can only be achieved by radical IT process changes that often spell trouble.

Cloud computing is not a product. It is a delivery model that enables the business to offer more services at a lower cost. Cloud computing is critical to the future of the organization. It will improve business agility, service delivery, customer experience, and customer loyalty.

We examined the adoption of cloud computing based on innovation diffusion theory. It became evident that many IT organizations don't really have a clear direction on how to choose the best strategy for cloud deployment. Which application is the right one to pick, that makes the most business sense, without losing control of systems stability, security risks, regulatory compliance, and performance issues?

Many organizations are challenged with the lack of accurate information, newly developed tools, and young, unseasoned vendors when it comes to building cloud strategies. Furthermore, many IT organizations have neither the details nor the documentation of their legacy systems.

Cloud computing is still in its infancy stage with many changes happening simultaneously. This makes it even more challenging to predict the true behavior of the application in a specific cloud environment, especially when it's outsourced to a third party. Latency, security, data synchronization, and other dependencies are some of the key factors in determining the end result of the cloud deployment and how it affects the user experience, cost model, and stability of applications.

Cloud computing is about striking the right balance between internal business processes, which is being in control, it's about keeping the data in house, in the possession of the organization verses outsourcing to a third party and not being fully in control of your own destiny.

However, the low cost to entry by many cloud providers offerings have accelerated the interest and the curiosity of IT organizations to test the cloud, and deploy an *ad hoc* methodology to test cloud. Many IT organizations experimenting with could deployments are building a non-production development environment to reduce
the time delivery window for development and testing.

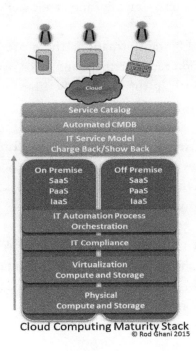

Cloud Computing Maturity Stack
© Rod Ghani 2015

Cloud computing further underscores the importance of building clearly defined and irrevocable strategic business objectives. By definition, cloud computing is an IT business innovation that must have a clear business objective; however, implementing cloud computing is a complex IT transformation that introduces risks to systems stability, security risks, data transformation and synchronization issues, ownership of the data, and unclear exit vendor strategies. IN some cases these risks are out weighing the promised value of cloud computing for many organizations, causing it to evaporate.

Successful case studies revealed that cloud deployments have a common approach, and that is the **commitment to a radical IT transformation** sponsored by everyone from the top executives in the organizations down to the line managers.

IT organizations who were successful in cloud computing deployment committed to building **new and separate environments with a skilled team** in orchestration automation. These teams maintained a strong emphases on service delivery and new governance processes to deliver services consistently, rapidly, and at a lower cost.

With such radical IT transformation, there are consequences, IT business transformation causes tremendous chaos within the traditional IT organization, which in turn causes the lines of responsibility and accountability to blur.

Cloud computing takes the traditional IT functions and turns it inside out, roles and responsibilities are overlapped, and there is not a clear RACI (Responsibility, Accountability, Communicate, Inform) ownership.

It's risky, yet many IT organizations are willing to take the risk, knowing that the adoption of the cloud will hone their competitive edge. It will also reduce their cost, increase business agility, and reap the true value of delivering IT as a service.

> **Cloud initiatives must be top down driven, starting from CEO and CIO level. The change must be assertive. It must be radical mindset shift. Every manual process need to be automated in order to deliver IT as a service.**

IT transformation starts at the customer's request, normally a service item at the service catalog. Service offerings must be clearly identified with delivery time and cost associated with the service.

Such fundamental transformations require a complete redesign of the IT service process. The service orchestrator is tool to automate required resources, deploy the appropriate requested capacity, manage and reclaim unused resources when the requester is completed with the service. IT automation is the foundation of a successful cloud computing platform.

Automation does enhance quality, however, it doesn't mean automation is quality control. Therefore, the process design team must ensure that the new processes have passed all audits and controls in order to deliver a consistent customer experience.

Cloud Systems Transformation

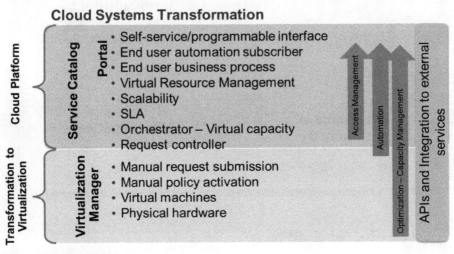

Source: Rod Ghani 2014

The successful approach to deploying cloud computing is for the organization to commit to a radical IT transformation to deliver IT as a service. Delivering IT as a services (ITaaS) is enabling a DevOps culture that's dynamic without silos between IT operations and IT Applications.

> **Cloud computing is not about giving up control. It's about controlling the service offerings in a rapid delivery manner that's consistent, accurate, and secure.**

The organization must have a clearly defined business objective and a detailed service management design, starting with a small initiative from end to end and then expanding the scope as the program matures.

IT organizations must start with a virtualization assessment and then build an orchestrated and automated internal process that can be delivered as a service via the service catalog. The infrastructure must be turned into a private cloud.

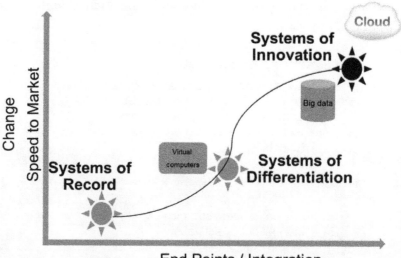

Source: Rod Ghani 2014

The IT organization must choose an application to deploy to the cloud; start by listing the entire application suite, and asses each application for technical requirements and business value. For example, Can the application be virtualized? Will the data be secure? Will system be stable? Remember, systems stability is number one goal to the organizations.

> **Understanding the difference between delivering IT as a service, not as a product, is critical to the success of the cloud deployment.**

Cloud adoption framework strategy requires a regress process and fundamental IT transformation, which must be sponsored from the top executives of the enterprise.

Develop a clear business strategy before purchasing tools:

Almost every business and IT executive agrees that, in order to build successful, viable cloud computing, there must be a clear and solid business strategy.

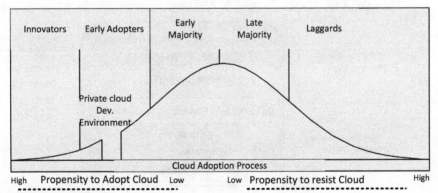

Source: Rod Ghani 2014

29

Cloud Computing Adoption Life Cycle	Innovators (2005–2008)	Early adaptors (2009–2011)	Early Majority (2012–2015)	Late Majority (2016–2018)	Laggards (2019–2020)
Internal cloud – Development & QA systems	21%	14%	21%	66%	77%
Internal Cloud – Mission Critical	19%	13%	11%	43%	65%
External Cloud - Non-mission Critical Applications	12%	18%	22%	31%	63%
External Cloud - Mission Critical Applications	6%	8%	14%	11%	31%
Hybrid Cloud - Non-Mission Critical Applications	8%	11%	17%	27%	30%
Hybrid Cloud - Mission Critical Applications	3%	6%	12%	13%	22%

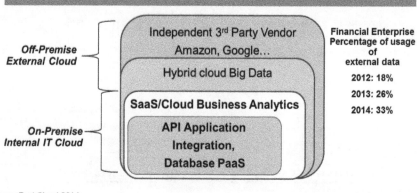

Source: Rod Ghani 2014

Strategy Guidelines

Preparation

- Select innovative team, out of the box thinkers
- Get the business involved
- Understand the business value
- Set a clear and measurable goal
- Set guiding principles to automate, script, and streamline the process
- Assess business impact
- Assess competitive advantage
- Validate application requirements

Business case

- Start with the end in mind, set clear business objectives
- Articulate clearly the value proposition
- Collect requirements
- Set a clear objective
- Build a project charter
- Build a governance model that will coexist with the new business process and manage compliance
- Build a business case, ROI model, based on external hosting vs. internal hosting.

Functional

- Select the application or the function
- Select a simple function – or application (not core to the business)
- Build lab environment
- Build new operations process
- Build a new dedicated environment (don't use shared or existing environment)
- Build integration points

Product Selection
• Bakeoff – product selection • Pilot selected product in a controlled environment • Request policy design • Vendor longevity validation • Build and exit strategy

Building a cloud strategy will require extreme discipline with a clear vision, essential to the enterprise's success and its competitive advantage. Anything short of this commitment will spell disaster for operations and application organizations. Virtualization using cloud is here and can't be avoided, but it can be delayed. However, the longer it's delayed the harder it will be to compete later and the opportunity to gain early advantages will dissipate. IT organizations must transform their processes from a product delivery to service delivery model, which is delivering IT as a service.

IT organizations must start with a solid cloud adoption by building the service model as the foundation to determine prioritization of which application can be moved to the cloud. This determination should be based on complexity, risk tolerance, and value to the business. Savvy organizations that take the time to create a solid adoption strategy can devise a road map that will allow them to take advantage of the cloud computing benefits while avoiding its pitfalls.

Cloud computing readiness assessment:

1. Business case:
    a. Do you have clear business requirements?
    b. Is the business aligned with IT's vision on the deliverable of cloud computing?
    c. Reasons for wanting to move to the cloud?
    d. Who is the business sponsor, and how committed?
    e. What advantage will the cloud provide?
    f. What happened if you don't adopt the cloud?

g. Will the cloud reduce your cost?

h. Will the cloud increase time to market?

i. Will the cloud provide business agility?

j. Is the business willing to change the business process?

k. Can the business handle the disruption of the cloud implementation?

l. How should your organization adopt cloud computing?

m. Have your organization determined which application to consider to be moved to the cloud?

n. Does your organization have a cloud strategy?

o. Does your organization obtain the skills required to implement cloud computing?

p. Have you identified and quantified the value of cloud computing?

q. Do have and ROI model on adopting cloud computing?

r. Do your organization understand the risks associated with cloud?

s. Risks:

   - Do you have a strategy to mitigate the risks?
   - Does the business understand the security risks associated with the cloud?
   - Is the business willing to work thru vendor challenges and applications performance issues?

2. Technical capability:

   a. a. Infrastructure:

   - Is your infrastructure cloud ready?
   - What percentage of virtualization is your IT?
   - What is the percentage of virtual servers compare to the physical servers?
   - Do you have redundancy built in?
   - How will you manage capacity?
   - Do you have the right monitoring tools implemented?
   - Do you have the automation tools in house

- How will you integrate the data with an external provider?
- Will you be building a separate environment for cloud computing or will it be shared with existing IT environment?
- PCI and compliance issues must overcome?

b. IT Process:
- Will IT be willing to change the IT processes?
- How automated is your IT?
- What percentage of scripting?
- Is your service catalog automated?
- Orchestration tools?
- Will you be charging back or showing back model?
- Will you have a back out plan?
- Do you have a DR strategy?

c. What type of cloud will the business need?
d. Will the cloud be internal or external?
e. How will you overcome vendor lock in?
f. Do you have the skills in house and the resources to support the cloud initiative?
g. Will your IT use a (Hybrid IT) broker of a cloud service?
h. Will your IT build a provide cloud?
i. Is your IT architecture ready to support hybrid and external cloud integration?
j. Is your IT capable to deliver IaaS ready?
k. Is your IT capable to deliver PaaS?
l. Is your IT capable to deliver SaaS?
m. Has your IT determined Service levels with the consumer and the cloud provider?

Research Survey Results

We received a total of 223 completed surveys from a broad range of company segments:

Titles	%
CEO	18
CIO	26
CTO	14
CFO	16
IT Management	26
Total	**100**

Financial Sector	%
Commercial Banks	12
Investment Banks	23
PNC Insurance	26
Life Insurance	21
Credit Card Services	18
Total	**100**

Company Revenue	%
Less than $100 million	24
$100 million–$500 million	18
$500 million–$1 billion	16
$1 billion–$3 billion	15
$3 billion–$10 billion	18
More than $10 billion	9
Total	**100**

Number of employees	%
1000–5,000	31
5,000–7000	26
7000–10,000	25
More than 10,000 employees 34%	18
Total	**100**

We examined the viewpoints of IT and business executives on how adopting cloud (or not adopting cloud) can help their organization become more competitive.

Depending on the business objective and the requirements, one can decide which would be the best cloud model to use. There is no one-model-fits-all.

The research focused on examining the reasons for the organization to adopt or not adopt cloud computing based on the innovation diffusion theory. IT executives base their decision to adopt or reject cloud computing on five factors: Relative advantage, complexity (stability, security), compatibility (integration), observability (Image of company) and trialability (easy to use, first to use).

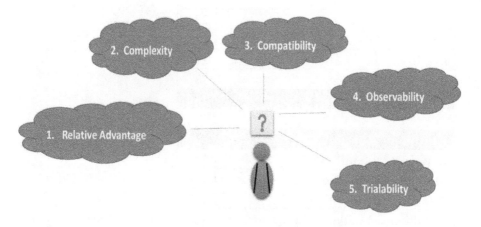

Cloud Adoption Decision Making Factors

76% of respondents use shared infrastructures or private clouds not only for Test/Dev, but also for production enterprise applications such as CRM, finance and Web applications. Of those, 30% are sharing resource pools between both Test/Dev and production applications, indicating a rising comfort level with sharing infrastructure within IT departments overall.

- 84% of IT executives would admit that cloud is critical to their competitive advantage.
- 78% plan to adopt a cloud strategy in the next 12 months.
- 81% said that financially they are able to support the purchase of the cloud tools externally or internally.

When asked if cloud transformation was going to be disruptive to the IT organization, 78% did indeed see this as an obstacle.

In most IT organizations that were surveyed, the technical staff and front line managers were willing to investigate and learn more about cloud technology. They were also willing to experiment and learn more about the external cloud as a new technology only. However they don't see it as becoming a standard business offering until they determined how it would affect their systems stability.

Many IT executives are not sure whether vendors' capabilities are sufficient to support and sustain their business. 42% of those surveyed were not as confident of the vendor's capability when it comes to hosting their own applications off premise.

The uncertainty comes from many sources, such as the complexity of integration points. Security and firewall communication issues, SOA services integration with external third parties, data synchronization, application performance, and vendor stability are all big factors in making the leap to cloud computing.

Business and IT executives are aware of cloud computing can assist the enterprise in accelerating time to market, and often it will lower cost of software licenses, maintenance, and human resources.

Cloud computing will solidify innovation, operation effectiveness, importance of security, intellectual property, and flexibility to deliver IT services.

Most organizations adopt cloud to turn their development infrastructure into a private platform with the objective of delivering a development environment rapidly. However, without a clear strategy that would be the end of the cloud initiative.

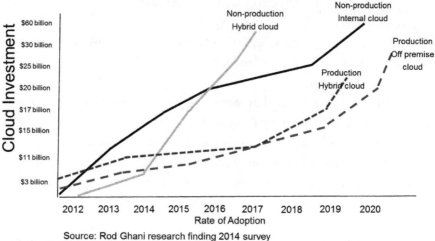

Cloud Computing Research Finding Executive Survey

Source: Rod Ghani research finding 2014 survey

Over 72% of the surveyed organizations stated that the reason for their interest in the cloud is to reduce cost and save money. The thinking is that the cloud providers are supplying a commodity, therefore it will be cheaper to rent rather than to own, which will in turn reduce capital expenditures. However, the external cloud providers may not always be cheaper. Additionally, external providers can put restrictions on standards that may be detrimental to the future of the enterprise.

More than 63% of surveyed participants indicate that they are currently using cloud computing internally and externally in a non-services impacting capacity.

The organizations are captivated by the notion that cloud computing will reduce IT cost and offer services on demand, enhancing the customer experience. Additionally, unlike traditional IT solutions, cloud does not require enormous investments in systems licensing and human resources. Cloud computing has a low barrier to entry, which has accelerated its adoption.

Most early adopters agree that the main drivers to cloud adoption are reduction in IT cost, scalable IT resources, and the ability to offer services more rapidly. However, company's data residing off premise and the outsourcing of IT functions are high security risks that must be dealt with and solved. Until then, these risks will continue to slowdown the adoption rate.

Few organizations consider cloud computing as a technical offering; however, the majority of surveyed originations agree that cloud is not a product but a radical IT transformation. It's about commoditizing product offerings and providing IT services via the internet as a commodity, 24/7, on-demand regardless of the location and the device at the customer end.

Many organizations deliberate that cloud computing may be the ultimate form of outsourcing and democratizing IT. With cloud computing, organizations can subscribe to a service and only pay per use as a utility model regardless of company size or financial capability. Some companies indicated that IT organizations may want to avoid or delay the planning and discussions on cloud computing if business units fear that the radical transformation may impact their jobs or even eliminate them.

In the future, IT services will be delivered by IT factories, much like our electricity being delivered by the power company.

Cloud computing's main driver is the multi tenancy (hoteling) model, as major economies of scale can be achieved compared to having IT infrastructure and human resources for each organization. Therefore, it leverages capacity more efficiently and requires less resources than the traditional IT model.

Cloud layers such as Infrastructure, Platform and Software can be instantly deployed on demand, as a service that can scale up or down.

Many organizations have accepted cloud computing as a strategic business initiative that must be implemented in order to survive and compete.

Most organizations have adopted SaaS for the non-business impacting applications. Most participants agree that the biggest obstacle to cloud computing is security concerns and not only about the lack of control but also the total lack of transparency. They believe, in order to speed up cloud adoption, more work is needed to improve cloud security, compliance issues, data synchronization, and systems stability.

Surveyed participants indicated SaaS deployments are the most common external cloud deployments, currently at 32% and forecasted to grow to over 50%, showing the most promising growth in cloud adoption.

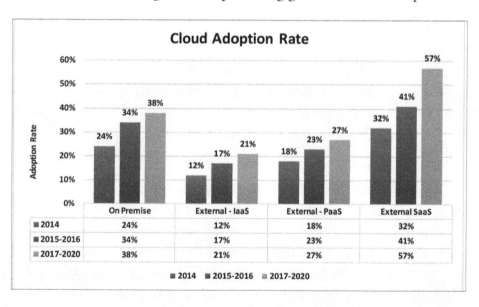

IT cost will drop as server virtualization continue to increase, as well as utilization density and higher efficiency. IT will experience excess in on-premises capacity as the shift to IaaS (Infrastructure as a Service) external cloud deployment continues to grow.

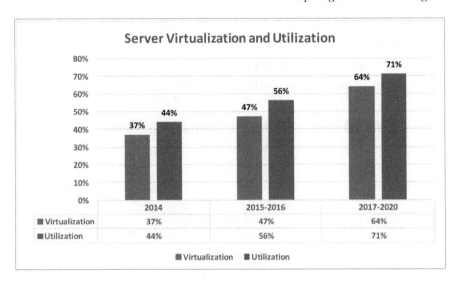

Server Virtualization and Utilization

	2014	2015-2016	2017-2020
Virtualization	37%	47%	64%
Utilization	44%	56%	71%

Those surveyed indicted that more than 35% of the organization's workload is being hosted on external cloud and forecasted to grow to 48% by 2018.

Amazon, Google, IBM and Microsoft are the top cloud vendors mentioned. A steady reduction of on–premises server and storage capacity is predicted, dropping to 11% by 2018.

Workload is shifting to virtual external cloud providers from the traditional IT physical server on premises. Participants estimate that, by 2018, over 43% of IT will be outsourced to external cloud providers. Additionally, virtual computers will be increased in quantity by 8 to 1 and will double in density in 2018. One of the primary drivers to cloud adoption is lower cost of servers, since several virtual computers can reside on one physical server. Also, virtualization density is increasing continuously, meaning more virtual servers can run on less physical servers.

Storage growth will continue to increase year after year as dumb devices become intelligent, and more data points are being generated. Location-based devices are generating an enormous amount of data about driving habits, point in time, health monitoring, alerting, and predicting, so called big data. Unstructured data like pictures and video files grew

2 times the rate of structured data in 2014. Structured data grew 16% from the year prior and unstructured data grew 34%, just one year. The work load is increasing regardless of whether the data is being collected on-premises or hosted externally with a third party cloud provider.

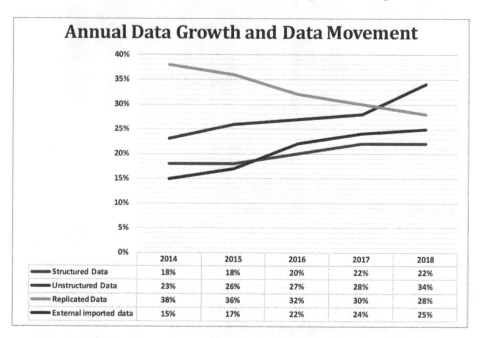

Annual Data Growth and Data Movement

	2014	2015	2016	2017	2018
Structured Data	18%	18%	20%	22%	22%
Unstructured Data	23%	26%	27%	28%	34%
Replicated Data	38%	36%	32%	30%	28%
External imported data	15%	17%	22%	24%	25%

The critical function has become not as much of collecting the data but translating and extracting the value out of the data, using is the data to understand and predict certain behaviors, making intelligent information that will add value to enhance services and become more effective and efficient. 74% of our participants said they are building big data farms, of which 53% are internal in their private cloud. 26% are working with a third-party provider to externally host their big data analytics function. Today only 8% of IT organizations are utilizing external providers to host their lower tiered storage for analytics functions; however, by 2018, that number is estimated to jump to 35%. Increased vendor maturity and enhanced security will attribute to the increase in outsourcing in the future.

Top five motives of cloud computing:

- 74% – Low cost efficient utility model – Pay only for what you use
- 78% – Business Agility – Easy/fast deployment to end users
- 73% – Monthly payments
- 52% – Encourages standard systems
- 64% – Requires less in-house staff

Key obstacles to adopting cloud computing?

- 54% – Data security, application performance and systems instability are the primary reasons for not adopting the cloud.
- 41% – Uncertain savings is one of the key reasons for not adopting cloud computing.
- 34% – Complex change to business process.

Organizations investment in cloud computing

Choice (%)	2012	2014
Have invested	11%	62%
Plan to within next year	13%	21%
Plan to within two years	21%	10%
No plans at this time	35%	04%
Don't know	11%	3%

Source: Rod Ghani research finding 2014

Survey Questions:

1	At what stage is your organization in terms of cloud adoption?	
	Discussion	6%
	Built a cloud strategy	27%
	Testing internally	31%
	Testing with external vendor	23%
	Begin used externally application hosting	42%
	being used – implemented internal (private cloud)	23%
	willing to revisit in 12 months	11%
	Not interested at this time	2%

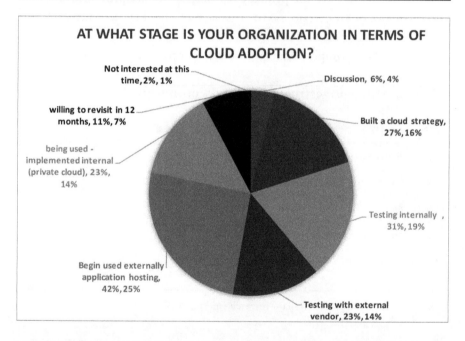

2	What does Cloud computing mean to your organization?	
	New technology transformation	46%
	New business model must be adopted	32%
	New way to outsource IT	13%
	Wait and See	3%
	Not clear about what cloud can offer	6%

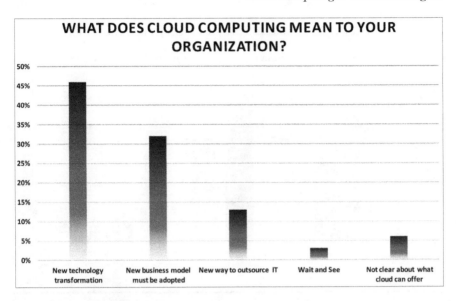

3	Which computer cloud your company is interested in implementing?	
	Private cloud	53%
	Public Cloud	64%
	Hybrid Cloud	8%

4	Which computer cloud your company has implemented?	
	Private cloud	41%
	Public Cloud	43%
	Hybrid Cloud	3%

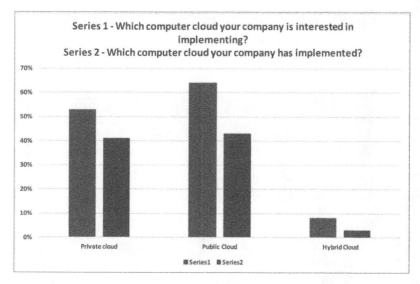

5	Which type of service are you using?	
	Software as a Service SaaS	34%
	Platform as a Service PaaS	25%
	Infrastructure as a Service IaaS	41%

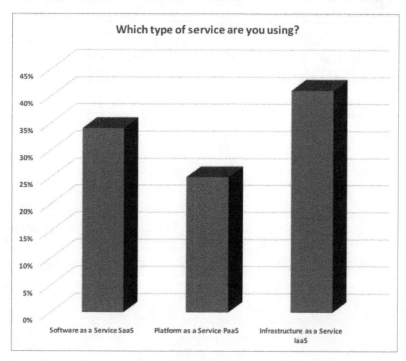

6	Which cloud base application function do your organization use?	
	Finance	15%
	ERP	16%
	Disaster Recovery	27%
	Server capacity	29%
	Office tools	29%
	Analytics –BI	31%
	HR	32%
	Project management	33%
	Email/collaboration	33%
	CRM	33%
	Storage	34%
	Sales	36%
	Marketing	41%
	E–commerce	44%
	Social media	52%

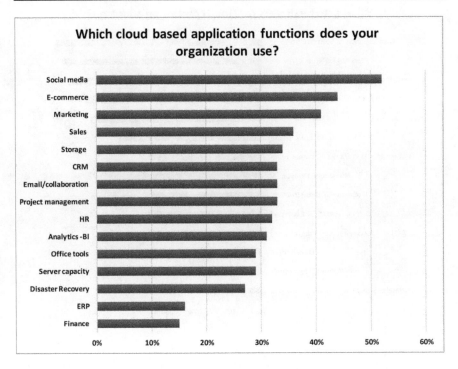

7	What are the drivers for cloud computing adoption?	
	Capital expenses to operating expenses	15%
	Reducing IT Headcount	23%
	Data Backup	24%
	Business continuity – Disaster recovery	32%
	Increase IT automation	32%
	Outsource IT infrastructure	33%
	No upfront investment	33%
	Instant provision for development team	34%
	Increase storage capacity	44%
	Faster time to market – Increased business agility	51%
	Scalability – Elastic capacity on demand	53%
	Flexible pricing – utility cost model	58%
	Cost reduction in Hardware	60%
	Cost reduction in Software licensing	62%

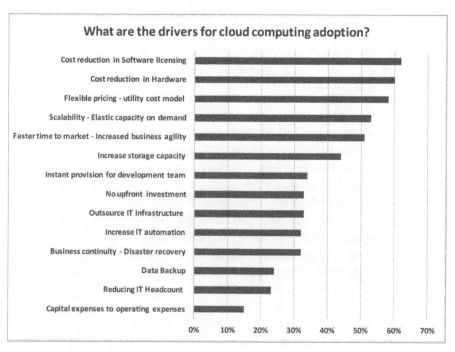

8	What are the most important factors when selecting cloud provider?	
	System stability	72%
	Data conversion	63%
	Vendor Reliability	55%
	Blackout plan	48%
	Price	45%
	Technical – Ease of integration	38%
	longevity – Reputation	21%
	IT support	18%

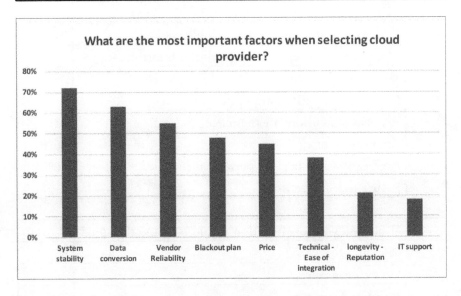

9	What are the main concerns in adopting cloud computing?	
	Vendor management and control	31%
	No financial value	20%
	Lack of standards among cloud service providers	23%
	Database performance	31%
	Vendor lock-in	32%
	Immature technology	33%
	Application virtualization	35%
	Data Synchronization	36%
	PCI compliance, legal issues, Privacy concerns	36%
	IT Business process redesign complexity	37%
	Organization acceptance and cultural transformation	38%
	Vendor longevity tenor	38%
	Network firewall – communication issues	41%
	Inconsistent customer experience	42%
	Application integration	48%
	Application stability and performance issues	66%
	Security exposure issues	71%

10	Who is in your organization would be using the cloud?	
	Sales and Marketing	55%
	Customer service	48%
	Business Analytics	51%

11	What functions of your organization using the cloud already?	
	HR functions	76%
	Sales and Marketing	32%
	Disaster Recovery	43%
	Email	33%
	Management reporting	33%
	Storage and archiving	38%

12	How much of IT's budget have you budgeted for Virtualization?	
	2012	8%
	2013	11%
	2014	13%
	2015	18%
13	How much of IT's budget have you budgeted for Cloud computing?	
	2012	3.1%
	2013	4.2%
	2014	8.1%
	2015	16.5%

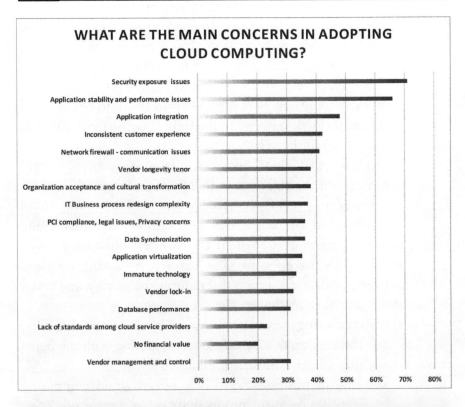

By 2017 the public cloud services market is predicted to exceed $244B.

Primary business drivers for cloud adoption:

- Business agility, quicker time to market to increase the competitive advantage through innovation and streamlined business process
- Lower cost, no upfront investment, utility based model, and on-demand scalable capacity
- Shared economy (Unused value is wasted value) such as Uber and Airbnb
- Big Data: Massive amounts of data being generated need to be stored and analyzed
- Mobile technology becoming more of a business tool to conduct business from anywhere, any time, on any device
- SaaS (Software as a Service) accounts for 56% of external cloud deployment. Meanwhile, IaaS (Infrastructure as a service) accounts for 31% of cloud computing deployments
- Nearly 40% of respondents expect to use a hybrid cloud in the next 2 years, and over 81% expect hybrid clouds to be the norm and core of cloud strategies in the future, surpassing public and private cloud initiatives
- It's evident that cloud computing is unstoppable and will continue to be the biggest growth segment in IT transformation. Businesses and self-empowered consumers are using cloud computing to outpace their competition. External cloud providers continue to sell to the business directly, with or without IT's involvement. The business is looking for rapid delivery, on demand service that reduces complexity, and better interoperability at a lower cost
- Cloud computing increases company and employee productivity:
  - Business units adopted cloud computing with the belief that it helps company productivity.
  - 72% of business executives agreed cloud computing increases company productivity by an average of 27%.
  - Improves employee productivity. 58% of business and IT executives believe the quick turnaround has improved employee productivity by an average of 20%.

- Adopting cloud computing results in a significant cost reduction and savings:
  - o 61% of IT executives said they were able to reduce software licensing cost by over 40%, hardware cost by 15% and labor by 20%.
- Cloud computing enhances the customer experience:
  - o Improved customer experience and speed to market are the biggest advantages to cloud computing.
  - o 67% of business executives said better customer experiences have increased their business by 5% or more.
  - o 86% of business and IT executives said cloud computing delivered IT services more consistently in a much shorter time. As a result, business users were delighted.
- Most organizations are building cloud computing as part of IT infrastructure transformation initiatives
- 72% of surveyed organizations said the top driver of cloud adoption is business agility.
- Most organizations are deploying private clouds to execute development servers' build-out.
- Business agility and quicker time to market increase the competitive advantage through innovation and streamlined business process
- Lower cost, no upfront investment, utility base model, and on-demand scalable capacity.
- Shared economy (unused value is wasted value) such as Uber and Airbnb,
- Big Data: Massive amounts of data are being generated that need to be stored and analyzed
- Mobile technology is becoming more of a business tool to conduct business from anywhere, any time on any device.
- SaaS (Software as a Service) accounts for 56% of external cloud deployment. Meanwhile, IaaS (Infrastructure as a service) accounts for 31% of cloud computing deployments.
- Nearly 40% of respondents expect to use hybrid cloud in the next 2 years, and over 81% expect hybrid clouds to be the norm

and core of cloud strategies surpassing public and private cloud initiatives.

- It's evident to that cloud computing is unstoppable and will continue to be the biggest growth segment in IT transformation. Businesses and self-empowered consumers are using cloud computing to outpace their competition. External cloud providers continue to sell to the business directly with or without IT's involvement. The business is looking for rapid delivery, on demand service that reduces complexity, and provide better interoperability at a lower cost.

Primary Inhibiters for Not Adopting Cloud Computing:

- Security and privacy concerns, regulatory compliance, identity theft, data being hosted off premise in a shared external environment is at a significantly higher risk than in the traditional IT model, where all the data reside inside the four walls and under the organization's direct control
- Allowing an external cloud provider to run the IT functions of the organization continues to be a high risk in the organization's mind
- Systems stability, data synchronizations issues, database latency are among the top inhibitors
- Cloud computing exposes privacy, regulations and introduces new security risks.
- Security and privacy concerns, regulatory compliance, identity theft, data being hosted off-premises in a shared external environment is a significantly higher risk from the traditional IT model, where all the data resides inside the four walls under the organization's control.
- Allowing an external cloud provider run the IT functions of the organization continues to be a high risk on organization's minds.
- Systems stability, data synchronizations issues, and database latency are among the top inhibitors.
- Cloud computing is not ready for mainstream:

- o Not mature enough to be in mainstream, mission-critical applications yet.
- o 68% of the business leaders said they will adopt cloud computing within the next 18 months.
- Cloud computing being considered for internal use and non-mission critical applications:
  - o 73% of the interviewed executives in business and IT said they are testing proof-of-concept and trying different technologies to build their own private cloud internally.
- IT risk:
  - o Data security, systems stability, and vendor lock-in are the main distractors to adopting cloud computing.
  - o 86% of IT and business executives are concerned with the data security residing outside of the company, and the systems stability relaying on an external vendor.
- Business process re-engineering is complex:
  - o 72% of IT executives said cloud computing business and IT process re-engineering is the most difficult transformation they had to implement.
- Fundamental organization cultural shift required:
  - o CIOs recognize that the most important issue to overcome is the traditional IT organizational and cultural shift.
  - o 88% of Business and IT executives said business and IT must come together as one unit when implementing cloud computing.
  - o 67% of IT executives believe that legacy applications are the most challenging transformation to the cloud.
  - o 84% of IT executives said that IT professionals believe IT job functions will be impacted
  - o Legacy application barriers, lack of documentation and visualization barriers.

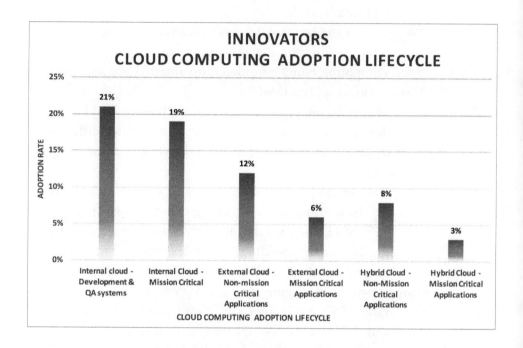

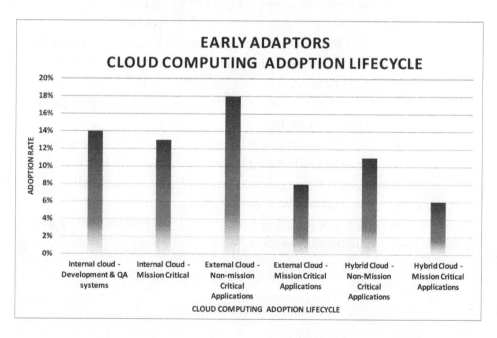

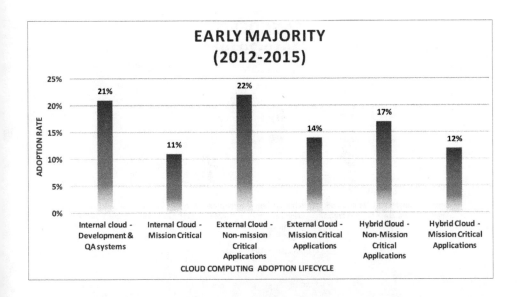

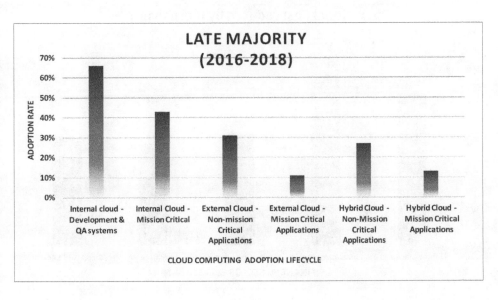

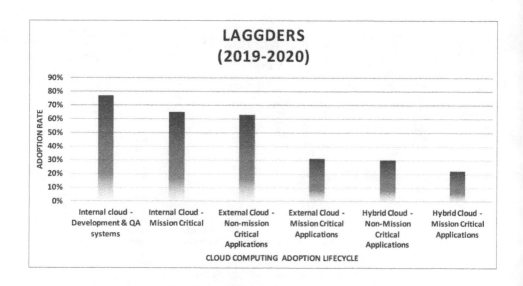

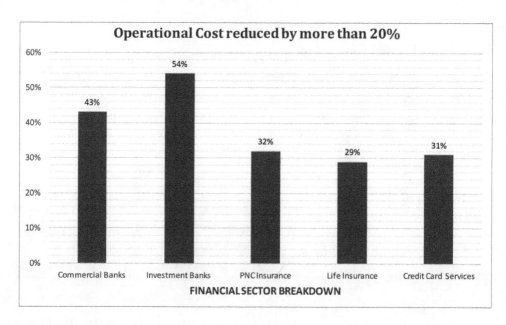

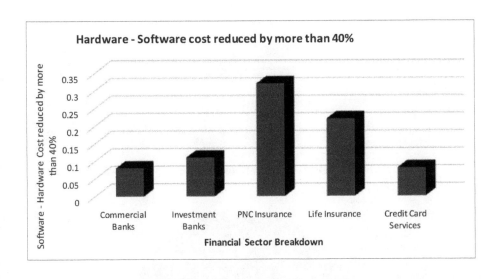

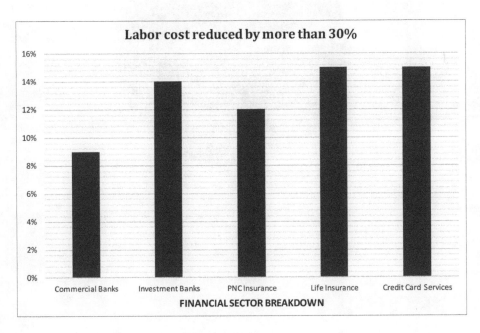

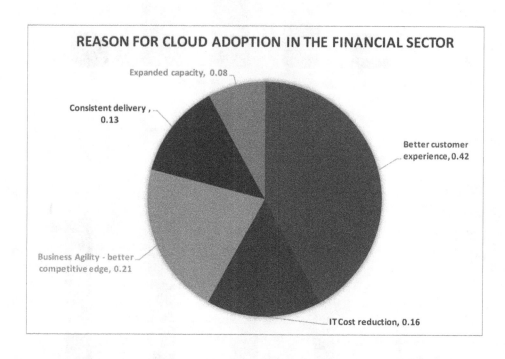

REASON FOR CLOUD ADOPTION IN THE FINANCIAL SECTOR

Expanded capacity, 0.08

Consistent delivery , 0.13

Better customer experience, 0.42

Business Agility - better competitive edge, 0.21

IT Cost reduction, 0.16

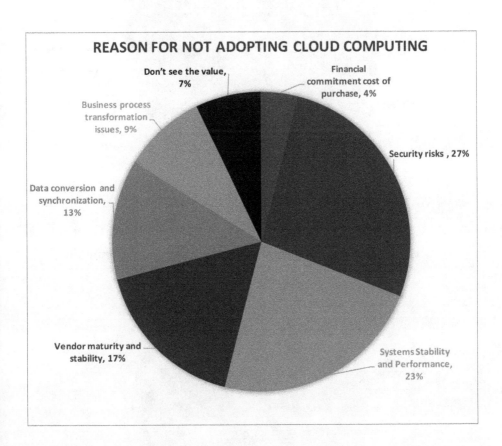

REASON FOR NOT ADOPTING CLOUD COMPUTING

Don't see the value, 7%

Financial commitment cost of purchase, 4%

Business process transformation issues, 9%

Security risks , 27%

Data conversion and synchronization, 13%

Vendor maturity and stability, 17%

Systems Stability and Performance, 23%

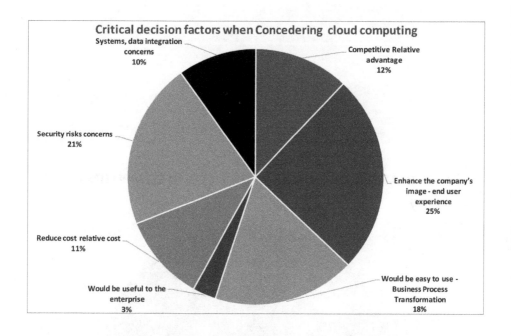

Critical decision factors when Concedering cloud computing

- Systems, data integration concerns 10%
- Competitive Relative advantage 12%
- Enhance the company's image - end user experience 25%
- Would be easy to use - Business Process Transformation 18%
- Would be useful to the enterprise 3%
- Reduce cost relative cost 11%
- Security risks concerns 21%

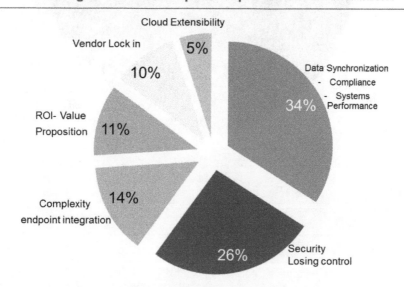

Research Finding Survey Results
Challenges of cloud adoption in production environment

- Cloud Extensibility 5%
- Vendor Lock in 10%
- ROI- Value Proposition 11%
- Complexity endpoint integration 14%
- Data Synchronization - Compliance - Systems Performance 34%
- Security Losing control 26%

Source: Rod Ghani – Doctoral Research IT executive survey 2014

Key Distractors To Cloud Adoption

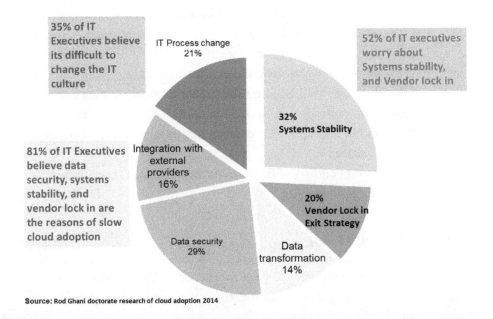

Source: Rod Ghani doctorate research of cloud adoption 2014

Research Key Findings:

- Public Cloud, Hybrid Cloud, Digital Services, and Big data will penetrate new market shares, reaching new customers and financial enterprises that will benefit the most.
- Innovation will continue to drive value and position enterprise to compete more effectivity
- Cloud providers will provide more unique offerings to meet customer's needs
- Business analytics and big data will continue to migrate to externally hosted status as the cost of cloud services drops.
- Core application integration points will continue to be the critical path to performance and security
- Cloud Storage will be highly adopted and storage will increase by 40% annually as it becomes a commodity
- IT operations will focus on business process and service management

- Cloud orchestrators will be the processing engine to control IT processes
- Service catalog and CMDB will become critical to the end-to-end service delivery engine, capacity, and managing resources
- IT organizations will transform to a service model, and traditional IT functions will become blurred
- Cloud storage will become the repository for big data and the new eco system data collection from external data points
- New cloud services will emerge and will create competitive differentiators
- Innovating vendors will fill in market gaps and serve industry-specific requirements

The bottom line:

Cloud computing continues to gain momentum. IT organizations see the value of adopting cloud and the risks of not adopting cloud. The main benefits of the cloud are:

1– Immediate services available on demand anytime, anywhere
2– Metered services
3– Efficient utilization of IT resources
4– Scalability
5– Lower cost

Estimated spending in 2014 on the cloud was $158 Billion.

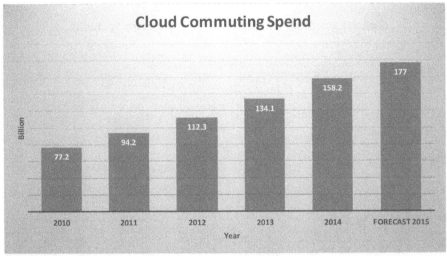

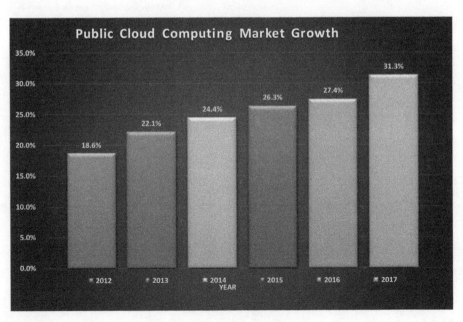

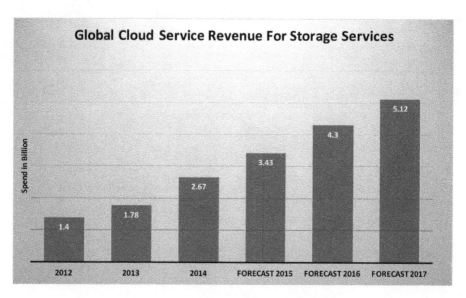

Source: ExpoTech Engineering Research 2015

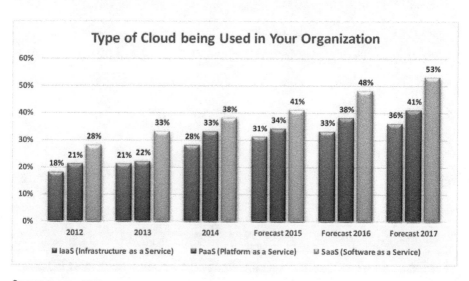

Source: Rod Ghani 2015

PART II

Cloud Computing Quantitative Study Methodology

The current, challenging economic conditions continue to press businesses in every sector to increase efficacy and productivity while reducing costs, in order to maintain a competitive advantage and meet stakeholder demands (Carlo, Lyytinen, & Rose, 2011). Businesses in the financial services sector experience increasing global economic pressures and a variety of growing operational complexities (Puelz, 2010), which require responses to take advantage of technology-based solutions that introduce efficiency and opportunities for growth. One widely recognized method of responding to economic pressure is the adoption of information management and technology solutions that allow the enterprise, or indeed an entire sector, to improve operations by capitalizing on its data.

Financial firms rely on data for their services, their business processes, and knowledge creation. However, regulatory, legal, and ethical obligations require that insurers obtain, handle, and maintain data according to strict standards, especially for security (Setia, Setia, Krishnan, & Sambamurthy, 2011). Recent advances in technology have led to improved tools and methods for the storage and manipulation of data as well as for the creation of knowledge (Howard, Anderson, Busch, & Nafus, 2009). One such tool is virtual computing technologies, also known as cloud computing.

In the 1960s, artificial intelligence pioneer John McCarthy proposed that computing technology be provided as a utility in the same way that a power company supplies electricity or a municipal water supply provides water; this approach to computing became known as virtual computing, or cloud computing (Sugang, 2012). Since 2005, companies such as IBM, Amazon, and Google have made significant contributions to furthering cloud computing technology, providing computing resources and services via the Internet, much as a utility company provides electricity via power poles and wires (Sugang, 2012; Wang, Rashid, & Chuang, 2011). This paradigm of computing services delivery is regarded by information technology experts as a critical but also potentially disruptive (Acgaoili, 2010; Watson, 2009) emerging technology that introduces innovations in both the delivery and development of information technology services (Wang et al, 2011).

Despite being viewed as a risky or disruptive technology, cloud computing provides a variety of measurable benefits to businesses, including the ability to enhance computing resources and capability at significantly minimized cost (Wang et al., 2011). This technology may be implemented successfully by businesses of all sizes and capacity, minimizing the need for the purchase of hardware and software and greatly reducing the need for technology support staff and management (Ryan, 2011; Sugang, 2012; Wang et al., 2011). Despite its affordability and the many empirically demonstrated benefits that cloud technologies may provide to the enterprise, many companies have not adopted cloud computing (Dlodlo, 2011; Fest, 2011; Jaeger, 2011; Low, Chen, & Wu, 2011; Ryan, 2011; Wang et al., 2011).

With increasing global competition and tightening economic conditions, business leaders who fail to steer their organizations toward successful adaption to change also risk negative consequences to market share and profit margin and, more significantly, organizational failure to grow and thrive (McKendrick, 2012). A critical aspect of adaption in today's data-rich environment is the adoption of innovative information management strategies that offer more effective and productive methods of data management and utilization (Wang et al., 2011). Management information systems and information technology researchers have examined the diffusion of some information management technologies within the financial services sector and in the Financial sector specifically (Berger, 2003; Kerimoglu, Basoglu, & Daim, 2008; Oliveria & Martins, 2011; Puelz, 2010; Setia et al., 2011). Numerous studies (DeWitt, 2012; Fest, 2011; Jaeger, 2011; Ruquet, 2011) have indicated that despite the demonstrated advantages of cloud computing, executive-level decision makers in the financial sector (Fest, 2011; Ryan, 2011) remain hesitant to adopt cloud computing. In order to better understand why Financial sector decision makers hesitate to adopt cloud computing, further research is needed to examine the correlation between decision maker characteristics and perceptions of technology and the adoption of cloud computing (Dlodlo, 2011; Fest, 2011).

Cloud Computing Adoption Life Cycle

This study addresses is the reluctance of financial sector leaders to adopt cloud computing technology, despite its demonstrated economic benefits, which represents a significant issue for both the sector and for technology providers (Fest, 2011; Ryan, 2011). This study will address this problem by investigating the impact of financial sector decision maker perceptions about cloud computing on their decision to adopt the technology. Specifically, this study seeks to understand the degree to which decision makers' adoption or rejection of cloud computing technology is influenced by their perceptions about cloud computing's relative advantage over alternative technologies, impact on company image, cost, security risks, ease of use, complexity, adaptability, or integration.

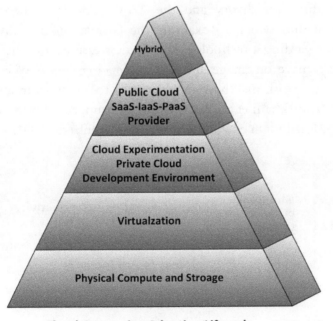

Cloud Computing Adoption Lifecycle   © Rod Ghani 2015

The purpose of the proposed correlational, quantitative study is to examine and assess the relationship between financial sector decision maker knowledge, beliefs, and characteristics related to technology and the diffusion of cloud computing technologies in the sector.

The goal of this research is to provide sector decision makers, technology providers, and future researchers with meaningful empirical data that contribute to the body of knowledge facilitating increased organizational results through the adoption of innovative information management solutions. The knowledge gained from the proposed research will assist sector decision makers and technology providers in making informed choices regarding the provision and the adoption of cloud computing. Innovation diffusion theory will provide the theoretical basis of the proposed research and an expanded technology acceptance model (TAM) shall be used to measure and assess decision maker characteristics and beliefs regarding cloud computing technologies. Data will be collected through an Internet-based survey of a representative sample of U.S. Financial company executive-level decision makers.

Innovation diffusion theory and the TAM provide a theoretical framework within which to examine the correlation of individual perceptions regarding a technology's usefulness ease of use, the effect adoption may have on image and the influencing factors of relative cost and security risk may have on the intent to adopt an innovative technology (Amirkhani et al., 2011; Chin, Johnson, & Schwarz, 2008; Davis, 1989; Kerimoglu et al., 2008; Moore & Benbasat, 1991.

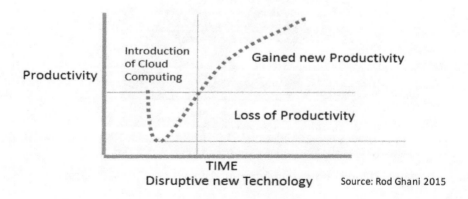

Measuring the distribution of technology is best achieved by using a relevant set of correlational factors (Howard et al., 2009). Enterprise owners and executive-level decision makers mediate these factors, as they relate to the diffusion of innovative technology in the enterprise (Liang, Nilesh, Hu, & Xue, 2007). Consequently, the attitudes and belief systems of these decision makers ultimately may govern technology acceptance, adoption, or rejection. Although external forces may exert pressure on adoption, they do not affect the behavior of the organization without first influencing agents of change (Liang et al., 2007).

In consideration of these factors, the proposed research shall be based on the overarching question:

How strongly do the characteristics, beliefs, and behaviors of executive decision makers in the financial sector correlate to the adoption of cloud computing technology in the enterprise?

In addition to this key inquiry, the proposed study will seek to answer the following research questions.

Research Questions

Q1. How does decision maker perception of cloud computing's competitive relative advantage to the organization over alternative technologies correlate with the adoption of cloud computing technologies in a representative sample of U.S. Financial firms?

Q2. How does decision maker perception that the adoption of cloud computing did or would enhance the company's image, end user experience, correlate with the adoption of cloud computing technologies in a representative sample of U.S. Financial firms?

Q3. How does decision maker perception that cloud computing is or would be easy use, business process transformation correlate with the adoption of cloud computing technologies in a representative sample of U.S. Financial firms?

Q4. How does decision maker perception that cloud computing is or would be useful to the enterprise correlate with the adoption of cloud computing technologies in a representative sample of U.S. Financial firms?

Q5. How does decision maker perception that relative cost of cloud computing is or would be lower than alternative technologies correlate with the adoption of cloud computing technologies in a representative sample of U.S. Financial firms?

Q6. How does decision maker perception that that cloud computing does or would offer acceptable levels of security risk correlate with the adoption of cloud computing technologies in a representative sample of U.S. Financial firms?

Q7. How do decision maker characteristics of systems and data integration correlate with the adoption of cloud computing technologies in a representative sample of U.S. Financial firms?

Survey Instrument

For each of the following statements, please indicate how much you agree or disagree by selecting the appropriate response from the drop-down menu at the end of each question. Please use the following scale: 1= strongly disagree, 2 = disagree, 3 = neither agree nor disagree, 4 = agree, 5 = strongly agree. Only one response per item is allowed.

Hypotheses

$H1_0$. There is no statistically significant correlation between decision maker belief that the adoption of cloud computing is more advantageous than alternative technologies and enterprise adoption of cloud computing.

H1$_a$. Decision maker belief that the adoption of cloud computing is more advantageous than alternative technologies is positively correlated with enterprise adoption of cloud computing.

H2$_0$. There is no statistically significant correlation between decision maker belief that the adoption of cloud computing will enhance the company's image and enterprise adoption of cloud computing.

H2$_a$. Decision maker belief that the adoption of cloud computing will enhance the company's image is positively correlated with enterprise adoption of cloud computing.

H3$_0$. There is no statistically significant correlation between decision maker belief that cloud computing is easy to use and enterprise adoption of cloud computing.

H3$_a$. Decision maker belief that cloud computing is easy to use is positively correlated with enterprise adoption of cloud computing.

H4$_0$. There is no statistically significant correlation between decision maker belief that cloud computing will be useful to the enterprise and enterprise adoption of cloud computing.

H4$_a$. Decision maker belief that cloud computing will be useful to the enterprise is positively correlated with enterprise adoption of cloud computing.

H5$_0$. There is no statistically significant correlation between decision maker belief that the relative cost of cloud computing is lower than alternative technologies and enterprise adoption of cloud computing.

H5$_a$. Decision maker belief that the relative cost of cloud computing is lower than alternative technologies is positively correlated with enterprise adoption of cloud computing.

H6$_0$. There is no statistically significant correlation between decision maker belief that cloud computing offers acceptable levels of security risk and enterprise adoption of cloud computing.

H6$_a$. Decision maker belief that cloud computing offers acceptable levels of security risk is positively correlated with enterprise adoption of cloud computing.

H7$_0$. There is no statistically significant correlation between decision maker characteristics of adaptiveness–innovativeness and enterprise adoption of cloud computing.

H7$_a$. Decision maker characteristics of adaptiveness–innovativeness is positively correlated with enterprise adoption of cloud computing.

The research employed several key constructs, which are defined below.

Smith (2009) observed that despite the widespread diffusion of cloud computing in the past decade, subject matter experts and researchers have not developed a clear, universally recognized definition. Using the definitions of several major computer companies and research experts, Smith (2009) defined cloud computing as "a means of renting computers, storage and network capacity … from some company that already has these resources in its own data center and can make them available to you and your customers via the Internet" (p. 65). This definition will be used for the purpose of the proposed research. The term *renting* in the definition cited above will refer to the process of acquiring goods or services in exchange for a fee.

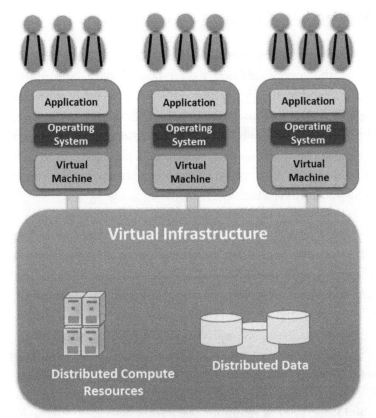

Cloud computing by Stack © Rod Ghani 2015

Virtual Computing; Also Known As Virtualization

Although the terms *virtual computing* and *virtualization* have been distinguished from cloud computing to describe the simulation of computing resources, including hardware and software, at a location (such as a desktop computer) where those resources are not physically present (Smith, 2009), in this research, these terms will be considered synonymous with *cloud computing.*

Accelerated Adaption of Highly Innovative Technology

Kirton (1992) identified characteristics of individual decision-making styles, observing that every decision maker falls along a continuum between highly adaptive to highly innovative. Individuals who are adaptive (*adaptors*) seek solutions based closely on established theories, policies, and practices. Those who are innovative (*innovators*) are more likely to pursue change when seeking solutions. The degree to which decision makers are adaptive or innovative is related to the rapidity with which they will accept new ideas and introduce change.

Innovation diffusion theory and the TAM will provide the theoretical framework for the proposed study's exploration of the relationship between financial sector decision makers' knowledge, beliefs, and characteristics and their adoption of cloud computing technology. Specifically, this theoretical framework will inform the study's examination of the impact that individual perceptions regarding a technology's usefulness, ease of use, effect on image, relative cost, and security risk may have on the intent to adopt an innovative technology (Amirkhani, Salehahmadi, & Hajialiasgari, 2011; Chin, Johnson, & Schwarz, 2008; Davis, 1989; Kerimoglu et al., 2008; Moore & Benbasat, 1991).

Adopting Cloud Computing

The Financial Sector

The internet has become a significant technological factor for many industries; however, the banking sector, much like the financial sector, has taken a conservative approach to adoption of new, innovative technology applications. Bradley and Stewart (2003) sought to determine the extent to which banks considered the adoption of online banking and the factors driving or inhibiting adoption. The study was designed using the theory of innovation diffusion but also considered factors of organizational aspiration. An online survey using closed- and open-ended questions was distributed to a panel comprised of purposively sampled managers from retail banks, consultants, academicians, and experts in e-commerce. The researchers identified and categorized emergent themes associated with the adoption of the subject technology. The results indicated that diffusion of online banking was due to the technology's ability to reduce costs and facilitate customer interaction. Factors within the banking sector that encouraged adoption were increasing competition, other banks' adoption of the technology, anticipated long-term consumer demand, and government influence.

Sector inhibitors were a general lack of innovative culture in the sector and short-term consumer demand. Finally, inhibiting factors related to the technology itself mainly concerned issues of security; in addition, the difficulty of implementation due to legacy systems, a lack of available bandwidth, and the rapid evolution of technology also impeded online banking diffusion. Bradley and Stewart (2003) showed that although online banking had been considered a radical innovation for the banking sector, the technology caused a significant improvement in sector practices.

Security, the dominant inhibitor in the adoption of online banking, was suspected as a reason that innovative technologies more generally have not diffused in the financial services sector at the same rate as in other industries (Bradley and Stewart, 2009). As an investigation of innovation diffusion (online banking) in a financial services sector (banking), Bradley and Stewart's study and its identification of security risk as a primary obstacle to adoption are directly applicable to the proposed study's investigation of cloud computing in the financial sector. The researchers' findings are particularly illuminating for Research Question 6 in the proposed study.

Other Industries

The exploration of technology diffusion across different industries presents several specific challenges to the researcher. Kerimoglu et al. (2008) explored the diffusion of enterprise resource planning (ERP) technologies across four industries by applying the TAM, considering also user satisfaction, user resistance, organizational memory, and environmental factors. The researchers hypothesized that among participant firms who had adopted ERP, perceived usefulness, perceived ease of use, satisfaction, and various effects of the technology were influenced by factors related to the technology itself, organizational factors, user characteristics, and several factors related to project management. Using surveys obtained from sector-leading organizations and other small and medium enterprises across the electronics, white goods, agriculture, and energy industries, Kerimoglu et al. used measurement constructs based on prior research and several qualitative studies conducted by the researchers. The results showed that participants who were satisfied with the technology attributed their satisfaction to the technology's compatibility and flexibility. The researchers indicated that future research may produce more meaningful results if limited to specific industries.

Decision Maker Characteristics

Decision maker characteristics and beliefs are known to impact technology adoption in organizations. Liang et al. (2007) observed that executive decision makers mediate factors related to innovation diffusion and that their beliefs ultimately govern technology acceptance, adoption, or rejection. Further, they argued that external factors, regardless of the strength, will not affect the behavior of the organization without first influencing the agents of change within the enterprise.

Chao and Chandra (2012) sought to identify technology diffusion factors among small companies through the lens of strategic alignment factors. The researchers sought to understand how alignment is achieved based on characteristics of company owners or executive-level decision makers, particularly related to technology experience or expertise, perception, and vision. Chao and Chandra hypothesized that owner knowledge regarding information systems and technologies influenced organizational alignment with technology as well as the adoption of technology. Manufacturing and financial services organizations in three U.S. states were surveyed. Regression analysis was used to analyze the data, with factor analyses and Cronbach's alpha calculations used to establish validity. The results indicated that owner or decision maker characteristics and knowledge correlated to the adoption of innovative technologies and perceived strategic alignment resulting from technology adoption. The study also revealed that although the rate of adoption of traditional information systems technologies in financial services organizations generally matched that of other industries, their adoption of innovative technologies lagged.

The research of Chao and Chandra (2012) is significant because it is one of the few published studies evaluating the characteristics of decision makers and their influence on the diffusion of innovative technology. The researchers demonstrated that the failure of an organization to adopt innovative technology may be correlated closely to low-level technical perceptions and a low sophistication level of decision makers, hindering the ability of the organization to use innovative technology to support its business strategies and goals. The researchers called specifically for future research to examine the adoption of cloud computing models in relation to small business and strategic alignment factors.

Cloud Computing Critical to Transforming IT

Cloud computing is regarded as a critical area of research in management information systems, yet the majority of published research is analytical or simply informative, with very few scientific studies, even in respected sources. Not surprisingly, many studies have called for additional scientific research on this topic. Harris (2011) discussed the many ways that cloud computing may benefit the Financial sector, citing statistics from studies conducted by solution providers and trade associations; however, this data serve little purpose beyond providing guidance for scientific research. Kenealy (2011) stressed the need for all insurers to move toward adopting cloud computing but cited the lack of sector and government standards for cloud technologies as a major inhibitor to cloud adoption in the financial sector. Unfortunately, Kenealy provided no empirical or scientific support for these assertions. Ruquet (2011) listed risks inherent in the adoption of cloud computing for financial agencies. Ruquet's research, published in an established trade publication, sought to advise financial organizations on a critical aspect of practice, based solely on quotes obtained from a technology vice president from Travelers Financial. McAfee (2011), a research scientist from the Massachusetts Institute of Technology, made significant recommendations for the adoption of cloud computing based on statistics from an IBM study and information provided by Microsoft.

Although analytical and informational research may be limited in its utility for academic inquiry, the recent proliferation of such research has provided opportunities for meta-analytical study of current research and the gaps that exist in information systems. Ahmed, Chowdhury, Ahmed, and Rafee (2012) explored cloud computing specifically as it relates to contemporary information systems research, noting that this technology poses some of the greatest research challenges known today. Ahmed et al. pointed to a critical need for future research in this area, stating, "There are still so many issues to be explored" (p. 207); however, they did not specify the specific topics to be investigated. Zamani, Akhtar, and Ahmad (2011) also addressed research topics related to cloud computing and made recommendations for future study that considered the inherent challenges therein. Some of the challenges identified by these researchers did indeed address technical issues and the importance of clarifying issues related to reliability, liability, and security in cloud computing.

Technology Acceptance Model

The advancement of information technology (IT) has permeated a wide variety of business enterprises over the past decades primarily because IT improves operational efficiency, lowers operational costs, and improves a wide variety of business processes (Lin, Shih, & Sher, 2007). The implementation and ongoing maintenance of IT is typically highly taxing on the resources of an enterprise, due to capital costs to purchase technology as well as the cost of the labor required to implement, support, and maintain technological enterprise systems. Consequently, enterprise principals strive to achieve optimal utilization of implemented IT systems within the operation, to ideally achieve the highest return on investment (ROI) possible (Grant, 2007). IT systems are traditionally most effective when used correctly and thus require the appropriate level of technological support in order to achieve that goal (Melville & Ramirez, 2008). Users will accept IT support systems only to the degree that the users perceive value in that support system and are ready to accept the technology (Ford, 2006). Consequently, the enterprise must approach the implementation of IT support systems with significant consideration of user training and orientation designed to facilitate users' ready acceptance of the technology.

Impetus Insurance Company (IIC) is a subsidiary of a large international insurance concern, based in Gilbert, Arizona. The company employs a staff of approximately 460. Half of the firm's employees are housed in the IIC corporate office facility. The remaining employees are housed in office suites located in neighboring office buildings. IIC uses a variety of proprietary software applications in the course of its operations, all framed on the AS400 platform using traditional delivery methods. Most of the enterprise's applications are integrated; however some legacy systems have not yet been incorporated into the overall enterprise resource management system (ERM).

IIC employs a permanent IT staff of 22, but uses temporary or contract IT personnel for special projects as needed. IT personnel conduct all operations relative to enterprise hardware and software, including equipment repair, installation, system upgrade, and system migration. In addition, the IT staff historically fulfilled the role of IT support on a case-by-case basis, meaning that if any IIC staff member experienced an IT problem, that associate would contact the IT department directly. If the IT staff member was unable to troubleshoot the issue by phone, the IT technician would go to the employee's desk location to further investigate and resolve the problem. Because more than half of the company's staff members were located in other office buildings, this process would often require the IT staff member to walk up to a block away. If the IT staffer required any tools or software to fix the problem, additional trips would be required.

After undertaking an efficiency study, IIC determined that this system of IT support was grossly inefficient, due to the amount of IT department resources that were required every time a company employee perceived that they had an IT problem requiring technological support. As a result, IIC implemented a company-wide intranet IT help and support system. Before any associate could receive help from an IT staff member, he or she was required to visit the intranet help system to explore possible solutions. Through a series of intuitive troubleshooting menu systems, the associate would be provided with a series of solutions to attempt, in order to solve their problem. If none of the offered solutions provided a fix for the associate's problem, the intranet system would log the associate's interaction with the help system and issue a case number. The intranet support system would then generate a report to the IT department, who could research the problem and report back to the associate with recommendations to resolve the issue. In addition, the IIC IT support intranet system provided an extensive knowledge base specific to the company's IT systems, including a variety of training tools to help associates expand their technological knowledge.

After a quiet roll-out, IIC's IT department put the new support system into use. After several weeks, the IT department reported that the IIC employees were not using the system adequately or correctly. A large percentage of associates, upon encountering an IT problem, called the IT department and requested assistance as they had done previously. IT personnel felt that they were in an awkward position when having to refuse to help, as their attempts to refer associates back to the intranet support system were frequently met with anger, resistance, and urgency. IIC invested substantially in their intranet-based IT support system, and sought the help of a consultant to ensure that staff members could recognize the value of the new IT support system and, as a result, properly put the system into use.

IIC's consultant explained to the enterprise the concepts of the Technology Acceptance Model (TAM), including Diffusion Theory and Technology Readiness (Chien-Hung & Mort, 2007). TAM addresses how, when users are presented with a new technology, certain factors will influence the user's decision about whether they will adopt the new technology and to what extent (Venkatesh & Bala, 2008). The factors of perceived usefulness (PU) and perceived ease of use (PEOU) are critical in determining how the technology will be accepted by the user. Similarly, diffusion theory (DT) evaluates key characteristics of a new technology to determine if users are likely to accept the technology (Melville & Ramirez, 2008). DT examines such elements as the relative advantage of the technology to the user, compatibility with the user's belief system, complexity of the technology relative to the user's ability, and the degree to which the user can identify the advantages to using the technology (Melville & Ramirez, 2008). Finally, the effects of technology readiness (TR) apply to the propensity of the user to accept and implement a new technology to accomplish a particular goal (Chien-Hung & Mort, 2007).

In his initial evaluation of the situation at IIC, the consultant first examined the support system itself, in relation to the relevant technology acceptance and diffusion theories. In order for a constituency to embrace an IT support system, the system must be both robust and agile in its ability to deal with queries because, if users perceive the system to rarely or never provide solutions, they will be unwilling to use it (Thomson, 2007). In addition, each time the automated support system correctly solves a problem, IT staff is freed up to perform other job functions for the associates and for the enterprise (Thompson, 2007). The consultant then evaluated the process required to submit a help ticket through the intranet to the IT department. If the process to request further help was too laborious or time consuming, staff members would continue to call IT directly or even attempt to divert IT staff when they saw them in the hall (Grant, 2007).

Next, the consultant evaluated the relative readiness of PIC's associates to adopt the new support technology. The consultant sought to determine why the associates were unwilling to use the technology, whether it could be attributed to a poor technological solution or to the simple fact that the associates were averse to the change in procedures (Booth, Laidlaw, Potts, Peppard, Rawlinson, Nagarajan, & Manwani, 2008). The associates polled by the consultant indicated that, under the old system, problems often were not resolved in an expedient or organized manner. This sentiment demonstrated to the consultant that the IIC associates were likely open and ready for a change such as the intranet help system.

IIC associates shared with the consultant that IT solutions often took more than one day to achieve under the legacy support system. They were generally unaware that, under the new IT support system, the IT department had established a maximum goal of four hours to achieve resolution of standard IT issues. The associates were also unaware that the IT department was able, under the new intranet system, to track technical support issues. Consequently, the IT staff would be able to determine if an associate's hardware or software systems were likely to experience a radical failure and could affect required repairs prior to the associate experiencing technological downtime.

Based on his evaluation of IIC's new intranet technical support system, the consultant determined that the associates' failure to put the new technology to proper use was not the fault of the support system itself, but rather it was because IIC had failed to adequately demonstrate the advantages to using the system. As a result, the consultant advised IIC to conduct a much more in-depth implementation, including training the associates in small groups on the proper way to use the system and how to obtain the maximum benefit from its features.

An enterprise will achieve the maximum benefits from any adopted technology when those who use the technology understand how to most effectively put it into practice. Users are most likely to embrace technology when they understand the benefits the technology will bring to both the enterprise and to its associates, and when the circumstances surrounding their job responsibilities enable them to be ready to use the technology. Understanding the way users accept technology as well as how the use of that technology diffuses throughout a population will better enable the enterprise to achieve its desired results when implementing new technological solutions.

Theory of Innovation Diffusion

Weber (2012) defined the parts of a theory as its constructs, its associations, and the states and events that the theory addresses. The researcher must understand the aspects and boundaries of a theory, if he is to work truly within the appropriate context. One of the most influential information systems theories, the theory of innovation diffusion, was borrowed from social systems theory. This theory, developed by Rogers (2003) initially defined the innovation diffusion theory parameters based on the innovativeness of a technology in a rural, agricultural setting. The context in which information systems places this theory may be drastically different geographically, but the phenomena around which it is applied – the effects of a technology on a potential adopter – is relevant in both cases.

Rogers (2003) originally stated, based on research he conducted in the 1950s and 1960s, that the adoption of a new technology is dependent on the characteristics of the technology itself, specifically the level of innovativeness inherent in a given technology. Those who have sought to advance Rogers's theory as it relates to management information systems have begun to explore the relative advantages an innovative technology may present to the potential adopter and the characteristics of the potential adopter. A variety of researchers have conducted studies based on Rogers original theory and have advanced its principles as they relate specifically to management information systems.

A critical component for advancing innovation diffusion theory involves the incorporation of the social system into considerations of technology advancement. Rogers (2003) addressed the technical systems of innovation and of the potential adopter. Bostrom et al. (2009) stated that, historically, researchers seeking to understand the diffusion of information systems artifacts in the organization focused too much on the technology at the expense of examining the social aspects of information systems. The incorporation of sociotechnical systems theories allows the researcher to examine both the social and technical subsystems individually but also their interaction with and influence on one another. The exploration of either subsystem exclusively fails to consider the broader dynamics of the interaction between technical and social aspects relating to the individual, the group, or the organization.

Early research in innovation diffusion theory failed to address the characteristics of adopters (or potential adopters). Richardson (2009) explored both demographic and perceptual characteristics of adopters of information and communication technologies in Cambodia. Originally, innovation diffusion researchers sought to understand how the attributes of an innovation influenced membership in one of several adopter categories, including early adopters, majority adopters, late adopters, and those who rejected the use of an innovation altogether. Richardson explored the influence of demographic characteristics on adoption patterns, and the degree to which perceptions of voluntariness or mandate shaped decisions. The demographic aspect of this research was critical in that it allowed the researchers to explore the ways that globalization determines technology adoption in less developed countries.

This theory posits that an innovation's market permeation does not follow a direct course but instead diffuses in waves that are successive and overlapping. Rogers defined five waves of diffusion, each with a unique group of actors; these groups, in order of adoption, are: innovators, early adopters, early majority, late majority, and laggards.

The TAM (Technology Acceptance Model) has been used in various contexts to predict the acceptance of a technology, to determine and evaluate reasons for the lack of acceptance, and to provide recommendations for how to improve acceptance (Davis, 1989). However, the model has been criticized for failing to provide a sufficiently robust analysis of the reasons why technology is accepted or rejected (Hsiao & Yang, 2011; Legris, Ingham, & Collerette, 2003). Although the TAM provides a basis for evaluating the influence that external variables exert on decision making, the model fails to consider how internal factors are relevant to adopter characteristics of innovativeness and adaption. For the purposes of the proposed study, the TAM will be theoretically expanded to include additional internal factors relevant to the intent to adopt the subject technology. These additional factors are decision makers' personal perceptions of cloud computing and their perceptions of the impact of cloud computing on company image. These will be compared with ease of use, complexity, and cost (the relative advantages of cloud computing) with regard to the degree to which they influence decisions about the adoption or rejection of cloud technology.

Using a quantitative, correlational design, is to examine and assess the relationship between decision maker beliefs and characteristics and the diffusion of cloud computing technologies in the financial sector. This section provides a historical overview of recent, relevant literature and research related to the diffusion and adoption of management information technology, decision maker characteristics, and cloud computing, with a specific focus on the financial sector.

Relevant literature and research has addressed factors of innovation diffusion, cloud computing, adopter characteristics, and the financial services and financial sectors in the United States. Fichman (2004) has argued that research in information systems innovation is critical as a driver of organizational competitiveness and is imperative based on the rapid advancement of innovative technologies. Current information systems research paradigms do not keep pace with the innovation-related needs of constituents, resulting in the need for a more aggressive and responsive set of research paradigms. Fichman described current paradigms of identifying and studying the ways and reasons that some firms possess the aptitude for innovation, essentially both the need for innovation and the ability to innovate successfully.

Low et al. (2011) explored the diffusion of cloud computing, albeit on a limited basis, in several industries. The authors surveyed managers of Taiwanese high-tech firms to determine the extent that an organization's decision to adopt cloud technologies was influenced by eight variables incorporating technological, organizational, and environmental factors: relative advantage, complexity, compatibility, top management support, firm size, technology readiness, competitive pressure, and trading partner pressure. The researchers used a logistic regression technique with each of the eight variables to test the model, observing the high potential for multi-linearity. Logistic regression, goodness-of-fit, and p-value data demonstrated that five of the eight variables—perception of relative advantage, top management support, large firm size, trading partner pressure, and competitive pressure—were positively correlated to the adoption of cloud computing. Technological readiness, compatibility of the technology with company values, practices, and needs, and complexity of the technology had no demonstrated effect. The authors stated that other industries are likely to have unique contributing and confounding factors that are not present in the technologically proficient high-tech sector; consequently, the author recommended further research in less technologically focused sectors (Low et al., 2011).

Although the Financial sector plays a significant and critical role in society due to the amount of money and social responsibility regularly entrusted to insurers by the public and other businesses, there is inferior knowledge about available information management artifacts and a distinct lack of innovator characteristics in the Financial sector, when compared with other industries using knowledge management technologies, such as pharmaceutical, biotechnology, manufacturing, and high-tech (Huang, Quaddus, Rowe, & Lai, 2011). This resistance of the financial sector to new technologies has been attributed to the significant financial, risk, and transfer-of-wealth implications of this sector.

However, as Puelz (2010) has argued, there is a tension between the sector's inherent conservatism and its need for an ever-increasing level of analytic and computational power. The author observed that the Financial sector has a well-defined business model and process structure, which has gained efficiency and cohesiveness over time through the use of technology. Puelz sought to quantify insurers' perceptions of the value of technology adoption, in this case, the use of the Internet and an electronic distribution channel ("online channel"). Insurer members of two trade associations were asked to rate the degree to which adoption of an electronic distribution channel had reduced cost, enhanced revenue, and increased customer retention. Responses varied based on company size, with smaller companies placing greater emphasis on customer retention and larger companies seeking revenue enhancement. Virtually all of the participants in this study ranked Internet technologies as having medium or high influence in their company's achievement of these stated goals. Puelz demonstrated the influential role of technology in the financial sector, particularly in marketing, underwriting, and claims, and concluded that the adoption of emerging technologies would separate "winners from losers" (p. 104) in the future of the financial sector. Puelz's results and their implications are critical to understanding the role that information systems play in the financial sector today.

A recent study by Amirkhani et al. (2011) identified factors that contribute to slow innovation adoption in the financial sector. In their study, Amirkhani et al. explored the aspects of the Iranian Financial sector that affect innovation adoption decisions related to mobile technologies. Concerns about the nature of radical innovative technologies and their ability to prevail in the long term have caused this sector to lag frequently behind others in adoption. Amirkhani et al. examined the TAM and its role in innovation diffusion in the financial sector, including the application of both technological and behavioral factors to the analysis. The researchers stated that previous studies had generally employed one set of factors and rarely considered both. The researchers established a theoretical basis for exploring innovation diffusion theory and the TAM in the financial sector, however, because of differences in the type of technology and the confounding differences of cultural and geographical factors, the study by Amirkhani et al. (2011) represents only a theoretical validation for the proposed project

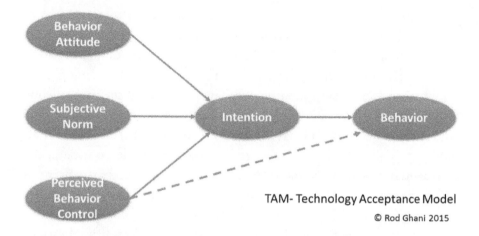

TAM- Technology Acceptance Model
© Rod Ghani 2015

Similarly, Amirkhani et al. (2011) applied the technology acceptance model (TAM) to innovation diffusion theory and those characteristics of innovation originally defined by Rogers (2003), including compatibility, complexity, and relative advantages. The TAM adds two dimensions of perception to adopter analysis of innovation, perceived ease of use and perceived usefulness. This research sought to understand the behaviors of potential adopters once attitudes and intentions are formed in response to an innovative technology, examining a variety of studies involving Iranian consumer response to personal computer technology, mobile applications, and e-commerce platforms. Amirkhani et al. emphasized the historical aspect of the theory of reasoned action as a precursor to applying the TAM to innovation diffusion research, noting that potential adopter attitude is highly influential in diffusion and is therefore a critical consideration for future research of this theoretical model.

Chong, Ooi, Lin et al. (2009) advanced the theory of innovation diffusion through the application of the technology acceptance model, the technology organizational-environmental model, fashion, and the organizational readiness model in an examination of how small- and medium-sized enterprises collaboratively adopted e-commerce in China. Each of these meta-models influence innovation diffusion uniquely; however, the interrelation of these influences becomes highly complex when viewing collaborative innovation trends in smaller organizations.

Prior research has addressed individual and single-enterprise technology adoption factors but the research performed by Chong, Ooi, Lin et al. is a critical example of how innovation diffusion theory may be advanced to consider adoption in a collaborative enterprise environment.

Bostrom et al. (2009) stressed the importance of examining meta-theory in information systems, which allows researchers to explore the constituent components of theory that are most relevant to the field. Without this meta-exploration, researchers may be unable to demonstrate how research findings interrelate across the broader scope of the discipline. Rogers's (2003) work in innovation diffusion considered little beyond the innovativeness of a technology, and not how adopter characteristics, environmental factors, or collaboration influenced diffusion. Technology and the phenomena that surround it have evolved significantly since Rogers first researched diffusion, as have the perceptual and demographic characteristics of adopters, potential adopters, and those who reject innovative technologies. Contemporary exploration into the complex interactions of these factors have allowed researchers in information systems to significantly advance the body of knowledge that can explain and predict if, how, and to what extent an innovative technology may diffuse in the information systems field today.

Disruptive Ecology

Internet computing as a disruptive information technology innovation:

Carol et al observed the innovation ecologies among enterprise are often poorly understood, and little research has previously been conducted that addresses innovation adoption from an ensemble perspective. These researchers theorized that companies adopt innovative technology for the purpose of benefitting from strong order effects, which explain why, how, and in what order that radical information systems innovations are adopted. Carlo et al surveyed 121 companies for the purpose of understanding why radical innovations are adopted by companies and to recommend flexible innovation strategies to a specific industry (software companies in this case).

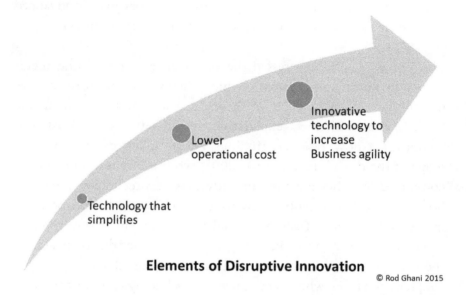

Elements of Disruptive Innovation

© Rod Ghani 2015

The companies surveyed in this example had adopted internet computing, and the researchers surveyed them with a paper questionnaire, sent to the top four executives in each company, to determine what other radical innovations they had adopted. They also surveyed their opinions about how radical they perceived three other innovative technologies to be. The researchers demonstrated through quantitative data analysis that radical innovations are interconnected and heterogeneous, and that those firms who adopted the subject radical innovation also adopt others, and those firms view the subject innovation as extremely radical. Chin, T. (2006).

Overcoming Resistance

Chin examines the widespread resistance among the medical community, particularly hospitals and clinics, to adopt current computing architecture and technologies. Electronic records and cloud or grid computing architecture provides the possibility for measureable improvement in overall enterprise performance, yet doctors and other key decision makers either resist the technology altogether or implementations fail altogether or in part. Chin proposes several specific strategies to overcome this resistance.

Although Chin's research specifically addresses the medical community rather than the financial services sector, the resistance challenges are very similar. While doctors and medical enterprise executives must consider the critical nature of patient welfare, their counterparts in the financial services sector must consider the critical nature of customer financial welfare. The resistance variables and potential solutions proposed by Chin in this research are relevant to the proposed subject matter.

Joseph, R. C. (2010). Individual resistance to IT innovations. *Communications of the ACM, 53*(4), 144.

Joseph examines factors that contribute to personal resistance to technology innovations. The research looks at various specific traits of non-adopters and the reasons for those behaviors. The research then looks at how the non-adoptive traits of individuals translate to enterprises of various sizes. If a key executive or decision maker of an enterprise is a personal non-adopter, this may likely lead to the enterprise failing to adopt technology innovations as well.

Management resistance to technology implementation represents a key variable in the overall failure of technology adoption and diffusion. Joseph's research details a source of resistance that lies at the core of the problem. Depending on the management structure of the enterprise, a small group of key decision makers who are technologically resistant may cause the organization to delay the deployment of technologies that would benefit the organization and its shareholders/stakeholders.

Lyytinen, K., & Rose, G. M. (2003). Disruptive information system innovation: the case of internet computing. *Information Systems Journal*, 13(4), 301.Doi:10.1046/j.1365-2575.2003.00155.x.

The concept of disruptive innovation applies to cloud computing architecture and related endeavors in a significant way. Lyytinen and Rose examine how cloud computing qualifies as a disruptive innovation and how, consequently, adoption of this important technological innovation may be delayed or disregarded by the enterprise.

Disruptive innovation or technologies represent a significant hurdle for modern enterprise, specifically regarding the diffusion of technology. Companies that are otherwise innovative and well-managed may fail to reach expected or possible levels of industry growth because key personnel, owners, executives, or managers may avoid the implementation of technologies that pose a significant disruption, even though the reward may potentially be significant. Using dozens of scholarly reference sources, Lyytinen and Rose propose several significant recommendations for overcoming resistance to disruptive technological innovations.

Markides, C. (2006). Disruptive innovation: In need of better theory. *Journal of Product Innovation Management*, 23(1), 19-25. Doi:10.1111/j.1540-5885.2005.00177.x.

Markides examines disruptive innovation from a dual perspective, evaluating business-model innovation and radical product innovation. Business-model innovation involves the process during which a going concern may develop a radically new way of doing business, while radical product innovation involves the adoption of a disruptive technical innovation. Each is examined from the viewpoint of the disruption in habit within the enterprise, and the traditional resistance displayed by management to these disruptions.

Markides' point in this research is that not all disruptive innovation is equal, and each must be examined within the context of the organization. In order to address and overcome resistance to disruptive innovation, it will benefit enterprise management to understand the difference between these two key types of innovation. Markides cites a number of scholarly works in this analysis, and provides a strong case of identifying potential innovation disruption in advance of the need for adopting it.

Thomond, P. N. & Lettice, F. (2008) Allocating resources to disruptive innovation projects: challenging mental models and overcoming management resistance. *International Journal of Technology Management, 44*(1/2), 140. DOI: 10.1504/IJTM .2008.020702

This research study examines four specific cases detailing management action and cognition as it relates to the adoption and diffusion of technology. Thomond and Lettice determined through qualitative research that management mental models and resource dependencies directly affected their pursuit of innovation adoption. The study concluded that mangers with restrictive mental models will present some or all of five specific disruption strategies.

Thomond and Lettice examined an area of technology diffusion that has not been widely addressed in information technology adoption or diffusion research. The beliefs and approaches of owners, executives, managers, and other key personnel form a significant portion of the enterprise's attitude toward technology adoption. Managers who are resistant to technology will hinder the enterprise's ability to compete in an international market where technology is a critical contributor to competition and financial success.

Emotions Drive Technology Adoption

Beaudry and Pinsonneault observed that, in technology acceptance research, most studies have focused on cognitive models with little attention given to emotions. The researchers proposed that emotions drive technology adoption behaviors and those emotions experienced by decision-makers early in the adoption process relate directly to use of the technology and the ultimate success or failure of its adoption. The researchers developed a study model that classified emotion into four distinct types and explored direct and indirect relationships between emotions and information technology adoption. The researchers surveyed 365 account managers in two banks regarding the adoption of a specific new technology and measured the emotions of respondents regarding their adaption to and use of the technology. They conducted quantitative analysis of the data obtained by questionnaire

These researchers identified that excitement positively correlated to technology adaptation. Happiness positively correlated to successful technology use however, surprisingly, negatively correlated to task adaptation. Anger was not related to technology use; however, anxiety negatively correlated to technology adaptation and resulted in psychological distancing from the technology. The researchers drew conclusions generally regarding the emotions of decision-makers and how those influence antecedents and acceptance of technology adoption, stating that the importance and complexity of these relationships should be considered in future technology acceptance research.

Fichman, R. G. (2004). Going beyond the dominant paradigm for information technology innovation research: Emerging concepts and methods. *Journal of the Association for Information Systems, 5*(8), 314–355.

Fichman stated that innovative technology diffusion research is typically conducted using the paradigms of dominant theory wherein innovations are proposed to be beneficial to the enterprise and wherein it is assumed that those companies with greater innovative needs will exhibit accordingly higher adoption behavior. Fichman theorized that these research paradigms have become insufficient and inaccurate for identifying contemporary innovation adoption behaviors and sought to develop new researcher models that may be more effective.

Through a comprehensive review of relevant literature, Fichman identified seven specific factors that he recommended be considered in future technology diffusion are:

1. Contagion effects
2. Management fashion
3. Innovation mindfulness

4. Innovation configurations
5. Technology destiny
6. Quality of innovation
7. Performance impacts

All seven were supported by the literature and research cited by Fichman. Using these factors, Fichman recommended a revised research model in which future researchers would consider the reconceptualization of generally accepted independent and dependent variables and the relationship between them. Fichman further recommended that researchers reconsider their traditional use of cross-sectional sample surveys and statistical models and instead conduct intensive, holistic studies of individual cases.

Gill, G., & Bhattacherjee, A. (2009). Whom are we informing? Issues and recommendations for MIS research from an informing sciences perspective. *MIS Quarterly, 33*(2), 217-235.

These researchers proposed that IT researcher faces contemporary challenges in identifying research topics and methods, in determining the most effective channels for research dissemination, and in obtaining the resources needed to support research activities. The researchers stated that contemporary research often fails to inform practice, focusing more frequently on advancing theory alone. Through a review of relevant literature related to innovation diffusion and cognitive factors that influence diffusion, the researchers sought to determine the source of these shortcomings and make recommendations for future researcher directions.

As the result of their research, Gill and Bhattacherjee (2009) determined that a focus on researcher publication was the primary reason that the resulting data fails to inform IT practice currently. The researchers recommended that researchers develop priorities for engaging practice on a discipline level, that academics and doctoral programs incorporate practitioner-level focus into academic programs, that programs be developed to place researchers into practical settings to increase their understanding of field-related needs, that elite journals publish practitioner-focused research, and that researchers develop practice-focused research strategies. Without these efforts to inform future MIS research, these researchers predicted that industry research will not meet the requirement of informing practice.

Howard, P. N., Anderson, K., Busch, L., & Nafus, D. (2009). Sizing up information societies: toward a better metric for the cultures of ICT adoption. *Information Society, 25*(3), 208-219. Doi:10.1080/01972240902848948.

Howard et al sought to identify the reasons that technology adoption factors vary widely across wide geographic boundaries and across large longitudinal spans. These researchers observed that it is difficult to study and identify specific technology adoption actors on a global scale or across significant spans of time. They stated that large-scale quantitative studies often fail based on economic variances in global markets as well as national policy, politics, or culture. These researchers stated that relevant literature demonstrates the importance of studying technology acceptance on a smaller scale of single, national markets; however, if this is not possible, Howard et al theorized that a research model could be developed using existing theoretical constructs that might facilitate international comparison of technology acceptance.

Through an analysis of existing literature and researcher, Howard et al developed a technology distribution index (TDI), which correlated the number of technology users in a particular country to the gross domestic product (GDP) of that country for a time period. This index was developed as a ratio of two ratios. The first ration compared a given country's economic output to all other countries in a given year. The second ratio compared one country's technology use to the technology use of all countries in a given year. The TDI index uses these two formulas to demonstrate whether a specific technology has diffused in a specific country in proportion to its economic productivity. Howard et al acknowledged the many potential limitations of this model, and recommended that future research further explore the potential of the proposed TDI model.

Liang, H., Nilesh, S., Hu, Q., & Xue, Y. (2007). Assimilation of enterprise systems: The effect of institutional pressures and the mediating role of top management. *MIS Quarterly, 31*(1), 59-87.

Liang et al theorized that top management within an enterprise mediates external pressure on the organization regarding information technology adoption and use. These researchers observed that the benefit of adopting innovative technology is not fully realize until adoption is complete and the technology is in full use; consequently research exploring the relationship between adopter characteristics and the benefits ultimately achieved from technology adoption may fail to identify the key decision-maker characteristics that led to adoption due to the time that has elapsed between the decision to adopt and the discovery of ultimate enterprise benefit. Liang et al undertook this research to determine the extent that top management exerts on technology assimilation, to determine how the beliefs of top management influence action in this area, and how existing researcher in IT adoption correlates to post-implementation assimilation in the enterprise.

Using a survey method to test their theories on how enterprise top management mediates other factors of technology assimilation, these researchers surveyed 100 managers of Chinese companies that had recently adopted enterprise resource planning systems. Quantitative post hoc analysis was used to evaluate the data, and the researchers determined that, although institutional pressures are significant in the assimilation phase of technology, top management influences assimilation positively despite the presence of these pressures.

Sein, M. K., Henfridsson, O., Purao, S., Rossi, M., & Lindgren, R. (2011). Action design research. *MIS Quarterly, 35*(1), 37-56.

Sein et al explored the disconnect in contemporary information systems research, stating that although design research should inform both theoretical development and practice, a quest to meet academic demands has prompted many researchers to neglect the practical focus of research. In addition, Sein et al outlined conflicts in interpretation between practitioner concerns and current methodological standards. These researchers proposed a new strategy for information systems design research that emphasizes the dual mission of the research, to advance relevant theory but also to inform industry practice and artifact design.

Through a comprehensive review of relevant literature and the study of one specific case in the information technology division of the automotive manufacturer Volvo, Sein et al proposed an action design research model, reflecting the researchers' theory technology artifacts must be shaped by organizational context. The researchers stated that the application of this model or similar principles in information systems research will help future researchers meet their obligations to not only advance theoretical knowledge but to also produce knowledge that supports practical aspects of information systems current or anticipated issues.

Taylor, H., Dillon, S., & Van Wingen, M. (2010). Focus and diversity in information systems research: Meeting the dual demands of a healthy applied discipline. *MIS Quarterly, 34*(4), 647-A21.

Taylor et al explored aspects of sociology in scientific research foundations related to information systems. Following a trend noted in current research, Taylor et al stated that research in applied disciplines such as information systems must meet both theoretical and practical needs; however, existing research has failed in many cases to agree on research priorities. These researchers sought to identify the focus of contemporary information systems research and determine empirically whether that research is meeting the demands of the industry.

Taylor et al conducted statistical factor analyses, using standard author co-citation analysis techniques, of a database containing all information systems research from the past 20 years. From this information, the researchers identified 100 authors representing a range of dominant subdisciplines. They the analyzed the database to determine how often these statistical experts were co-cited by other authors and to establish relational links between groups of authors. Using an analysis of continuity and change over the 20 year period, Taylor et al evaluated focus and diversity in the field across that temporal span. The researchers identified research trends that demonstrated aspects of disintegration, isolation, and stagnation in the body of IS research. They recommended that future researchers in the industry focus on interdisciplinary approaches that will research to respond quickly and relevantly to the rapidly changing field of information systems.

Embracing New Technology

Carmen, R., & Diana, C. (2009). Business integration. *Annals of the University of Oradea, Economic Science Series, 18*(4), 1035.

This research details the rapid and significant ways that data exchange has changed and how these changes affect the enterprise. Carmen and Diana examine how electronic and technological innovation has overcome the barriers to success that many companies previously encountered. Despite these innovations, many enterprises have hesitated to adopt new technologies because companies often fail to keep up with what technology is available and how that technology can truly benefit the organization.

Although Carmen and Diana fail to offer any practical solutions for how the enterprise might overcome resistance to integration and thus enjoy maximum industry success, this research presents a detailed explanation of many of the reasons companies do hesitate to adopt new technology. This research details several areas of resistance often overlooked in other resources, including dependency issues and the lack of discipline and standards found in many enterprises.

Cavusoglu, H., Hu, N., Li, Y., & Ma, D. (2010). Information technology diffusion with influentials, imitators, and opponents.

Rod Kamal Ghani Agha, Ph.D.

Journal of Management Information Systems, 27(2), 305–334. Doi:10.2753/
MIS0742-1222270210

These researchers stated that innovative technologies follow diverse
diffusion patterns and that these patterns follow a two-segment model
of potential adopters. They theorized that, in the two-segment model
previously addressed by researchers, the influential tendencies of
adopter promotion had been addressed; however, prior research had
not examined that segment of society that exerted a negative influence
on potential adopters. Cavusoglu et al proposed to examine information
technology innovation diffusion using a three-segment model, from
the perspective of three types of actors within the target population of
the innovation. Those types of actors were influencers, opponents, and
imitators. The stated goal of this research was to identify information
that will allow enterprise to identify and predict segments of adopters
based on the influencers.

Using data sets from nine prior research projects found in the literature,
Cavusoglu et al tested their three-segment model to a diverse set of
innovations, including medical equipment, home appliances, and
agricultural products. The researchers examined each of the nine cases
using model performance comparisons and also produced simulation
analyses to further test the model. They determined that, in several of
the subject cases, the two-segment model returned data that may be
misleading. They concluded that influencers and opponents have an
asymmetric influence on the innovation behaviors of imitators, however
imitators exert no influence on the other two. This model demonstrated
an effective predictor for innovation adoption when a large opponent
contingent exists, and identified diffusion patters for three distinct
segments of technology, predicting future adoption trends.

Davis, F. D. (1989). Perceived usefulness, perceived ease of use, and user
acceptance of information technology. *MIS Quarterly, 13*(3), 319–340.

Davis observed that a lack of measurement instruments existed for
predicting user acceptance of computer technologies, and that those

measurements that did exist lacked any demonstrable validity. Davis further observed that existing measurements failed to consider usage of the technology after adoption. This researcher sought to develop and validate two scales for measuring perceived usefulness of a technology and perceived ease of use of that technology. These scales were developed by Davis using demonstrated and accepted theories of technology diffusion in the management information systems field.

Using existing research, Davis developed 14 candidate items to be included in the instrument. The research consisted of pre-test interviews and two separate field test studies wherein the candidate items were presented in questionnaires to technology users. After each phase, Davis tested for reliability and internal validity through data analysis, and eliminated those items that did not sufficient demonstrate valid and reliable results. Davis observed that user reactions to technology are complex and multifaceted, and that the systematic research of those factors that drive user behavior provides the best opportunity reliable measures for the critical examination of theoretical models.

Kee-Young, K., & Hee-Woong, K. (2008). Managing readiness in enterprise systems–driven organizational change. *Behaviour & Information Technology, 27*(1), 79.Doi:10.1080

This research project details the complexity of adopting enterprise systems in the enterprise and outlines strategies on how to best prepare for the significant organizational changes that occur through the adoption of innovative enterprise technology. Kee-Young and Hee-Woong examine issues of readiness and conclude that the key to readiness is the overcoming of resistance. The research model for this study included collecting data from the clients of one solution provider who agreed to sponsor the study. The study poses a new construct, readiness for change, as it relates to information system adoption and details the factors crucial for adopter readiness.

This extensive research project finds its basis in a large number of prior studies and research analyses, and each is cited as a scholarly resource.

The results obtained by Kee-Young and Hee-Woong clearly illustrate several ways to address technological resistance in the enterprise. The authors support their conclusion that the concept of readiness for change may significantly mitigate enterprise solution implementation failure. These concepts may be applied directly to the subject area of implementation and diffusion of cloud computing architecture and technology.

Practical Applications of Innovation Adoption

The concept of theory finds its history in the most basic philosophical concepts, seeking to explain abstract models of human thought and behavior. The scientific application of theory to practice seeks to expand the definition of abstract concepts and apply them to observed or conceptualized phenomena. In the management information systems discipline, theoretical development and the application of theory to practice often lags behind the rapid advancement of technology and its implementation (Gregor, 2006). To forestall this trend of the allegorical cart leading the horse, contemporary information systems researchers have sought to develop or advance theory in ways that are meaningful for those who practice in the field. Borrowing from social and behavioral theorists, researchers have pursued the development of innovation diffusion theory to explain or predict phenomena related to information systems and to prescribe aspects of practice that may advance the discipline.

In those disciplines with extensive histories, the application of theory to practice has been undertaken for perhaps centuries. In the information systems discipline, which has existed for only a few decades, the practice is relatively new and regarded by many experts as not particularly effective. Bostrom and Heinen (1977) were among the first information systems researchers who demonstrated the application of theory in an organizational setting, albeit hypothetically. In the case presented here, the circulation department of a large newspaper was in need of process redesign. Bostrom and Heinen proposed the application of socio-technical systems (STS) theory to create a flexible work/

information system that could adapt to the changing nature and needs of the operation. The application of STS theory in this case considered the secondary changes that would result in other departments as a result of streamlining processes in the circulation unit.

More than three decades after Bostrom and Heinen (1977) utilized theory in a practical application, Bostrom, Gupta, and Thomas (2009) observed that, although information systems research had developed a significant number of theories, little had been done in practice to apply them. Although information systems approaches are used ubiquitously to increase efficiency and results in an organizational context, the majority of emphasis is placed on technology rather than theory. Bostrom et al. revisited the importance of using STS and related theories as a lens through which to view the needs of the organization and the potential effects that the integration of different information systems paradigms may cause. Bostrom et al. strongly recommended further research in this area as well as in meta-theories of information systems, to increase awareness in the field regarding the importance of theoretical integration with practice.

In some research, the retrospective application of theory to specific phenomena may help explain those events. Goldberg, Lowengart, Oreg, and Bar-Eli (2010) examined the diffusion of radical innovation from a management perspective using the history of the Fosbury Flop. Fosbury, an American athlete, revolutionized his sport through the introduction of a radical technique that proved to be significantly superior to previous techniques. Consequently, the technique was adopted universally in the sport in less than a decade. In the organizational setting, this analogy demonstrated that innovations do not necessarily develop in response to a specific or substantial need; rather, many emerge without an initial demand. Goldberg et al. explored this phenomenon from the perspective of potential innovators, which is a perspective few researchers adopt. A significant need exists in the information systems body of research for further exploration of innovation diffusion from the viewpoint of the visionary.

If individual disciplines or fields rely on scientific research to further relevant theory, the thematic choices made by researchers have the potential to ultimately, albeit indirectly, influence practice. Constantinides, Chiasson, and Introna (2012) analyzed the theoretical and methodological choices that information systems researchers make and how those choices influence the state of the field. Academics and subject matter experts argue that a sizeable gap exists between research relevance and practice in information systems. Recommended solutions to this problem include making research more consumable by practitioners, creating more implementable knowledge, and using applicability checks to determine relevance. This discussion calls into question the intentions of information systems researchers and what audience they seek to serve. The imperative to publish must never override the obligation to serve society; yet many researchers select topics and design research based on the inclinations of leading journals. Even if research has rigor, it fails to serve its constituents if it lacks relevance. Constantinides et al. recommended a pragmatic framework for orienting researchers individually and collectively toward a greater interest in the ends of information systems research, such that the direction of theoretical development might eventually converge with practical application.

Although theory can be advanced without practical application, this practice may be ill-advised in an applied discipline such as information systems. Miller and Tsang (2011) examined both the practical and philosophical hurdles to testing theories through practical application. The challenge inherent in testing this class of theory relates to the field's reliance on correlational data in lieu of direct evidence. Researchers have little opportunity to test relevant theory in a real-world application because the implications on an operating enterprise may be significant and likely unethical. Nevertheless the field, already lacking academic relevance, continues to suffer from a lack of theoretical rigor. To improve the theoretical health of the discipline and ease the difficulty in applying theory to practice, Miller and Tsang recommended a careful review of research designs, discontinued over-reliance on untested assumptions, and a paradigm shift in the epistemological stance that has previously dominated information systems research.

Many aspects of information systems research involves human behavior, either in organizational context or as individual consumers; consequently, it is logical to assume that behaviorist theories may have direct relevance in the field. Richardson (2009) applied innovation diffusion theory in an attempt to identify characteristics of those who exhibited adopter behavior versus non-adopter behavior in response to technology adoption. A particularly valuable and illustrative result of this research was that the younger and more experienced research participants perceived greater advantage in the subject technology. Practitioners in the information systems field are often surprised or confounded when system implementations fail at the organizational level. Richardson's research is a critical example of how the application of theory may assist in practical scenarios.

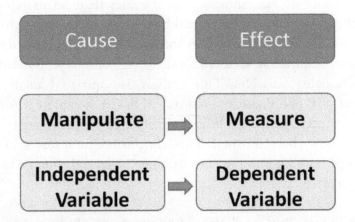

In a relatively new field of study such as information systems, researchers often struggle to determine whether theories may endure. This challenge is further complicated by the mercurial and rapidly changing nature of the field. As the technologies that underlie the information systems field evolve, it may be difficult for theoretical development and testing to keep pace. Grant (2010) examined the knowledge management theory, observing that many researchers and academics regard it as a passing theoretical fad rather than an enduring base on which to build knowledge. Grant's research demonstrated mixed results on the enduring nature of knowledge management (KM) theory, stating that a "next generation" (p. 216) phase of KM may compensate for some of the inadequacies detected in its older iterations. The more important question for information systems researchers however may be one of meta-analysis. In other words, does the information systems discipline need theories that pass in and out of effectiveness as quickly as the artifacts of the field?

The innovation diffusion theoretical model has been advanced in many cases through its application when paired with other theories or models. Amirkhani, Salehahmadi, Kheiri, and Hajialiasgari (2011) examined the theory of reasoned action and the technology acceptance model (TAM) as they relate to innovation diffusion. The TAM examines perceived ease of use and perceived usefulness as influencers on technology artifact diffusion, adding a critical component to Rogers's (2003) focus on the characteristics of the innovation itself rather than on its interaction with the potential adopter. Amirkhani et al. identified factors that influence information technology diffusion including knowledge of an innovation, education, socioeconomic status, communication behavior, and personality variables. This analysis demonstrated an important aspect of diffusion that many researchers have not explored: Adoption may vary greatly among different groups of adopters, regardless of the artifact's characteristics. This conclusion indicates a need for additional research into the correlation between diffusion and adopter characteristics.

Chong, Ooi, Tak, and Yang (2009) explored the adoption of e-commerce technologies in China's textile sector as a means of increasing competitiveness. Noting that many small- and medium-sized enterprises (SMEs) in this sector have not adopted the technology despite its accessibility and demonstrated efficacy for increasing viability, these researchers sought to identify reasons for non-adoption. The findings reported by Chong, Ooi, Tak et al. indicated that a combination of organizational readiness, enterprise innovativeness, and organizational culture created a scenario in which the enterprise was likely to adopt e-commerce technology. Chong, Ooi, Tak et al. classified e-commerce in this research as an innovative technology with which few SME participants were familiar. Further and more extensive research following this model has the capacity to advance relevant theory or introduce new theoretical models, as patterns emerge and the interaction of factors is demonstrated as applicable in many cases.

Chong, Ooi, Lin, and Raman (2009) furthered the research performed by Chong, Ooi, Tak et al. (2009), studying collaborative electronic commerce (c-commerce) adoption factors in the electronics sector in Malaysia. C-commerce differs from existing information systems platforms, facilitating electronic collaboration with trading partners (also known as a collaborative supply chain through the use of c-commerce) and requiring technology adoption by more than one enterprise and the enterprise's adoption of an information sharing culture. Consequently, this technology is classified as innovative for the purpose of the subject research. The researchers demonstrated implications that are significant to the theoretical relationship between adoption factors and innovative technologies, specifically c-commerce. In this study, companies adopted the technology largely due to competitive and governance-related pressures within the sector and pressure from existing and potential trading partners. Enterprises were more willing to adopt c-commerce if there was an information interpretation in process, supporting at least two key mini-theories associated with innovation diffusion.

Predicting complex program outputs historically has posed a challenge for researchers based on the countless factors involved. Reed and Jordan (2007) used Rogers's (2003) theory of innovation diffusion as a framework for analyzing program outcomes of energy efficiency and renewable energy (EERE) technologies. In the subject example, agencies seek the diffusion of EERE programs for the purpose of influencing adopter behavior to change. Although consumer incentives are typically offered for participation, Reed and Jordan determined that incentives are not sufficient to ensure diffusion. This research demonstrated a high degree of complexity in the interaction among programs, sponsors, adopters, and influencers but was successful in predicting outcomes using the logic model and the innovation diffusion theory applied to multiple actors in the scenario. This research is highly relevant to numerous disciplines that may benefit from the ability to predict diffusion relative to programs of all types.

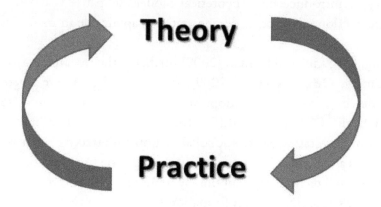

The relationship between theory and practice is highly complex in any field; however, in business and management this translation becomes an even greater challenge as practical application may take many diverse forms. The management information systems subdiscipline is relatively new in terms of theory development and, as a result, the field has borrowed many of its major theoretical paradigms from other fields (Gregor, 2006). Relevant literature identifies the genesis of information systems as a formalized discipline as occurring in the latter half of the 1970s (Gregor 2006; Avison & Elliot, 2005). The formal development of theoretical thought in information systems has followed a variety of diverse paths, methods, and approaches, none of which is generally considered to be the dominant or guiding standard.

Technology Adoption   Source: Rod Ghani 2015

So scattered are the theoretical underpinnings of information systems that Gregor (2006) explored the ontological character and basis for theoretical development, stating that, although many information systems researchers use the word *theory* in their work, they neglect to provide any governing definition or explanation of what they consider the nature of theory to be. Generally, information systems literature and research provide prescriptions for practice that encompass operational methods and paradigms that are believed or demonstrated through research to possess a higher level of efficacy than the alternatives. If no clear or recognized set of theoretical principles exist in relation to information systems, reasons for the generally recognized disconnection between theory and practice in the field become evident.

The information systems researcher faces a difficult task in light of this discipline-related ontological deficiency. Scientific research relies on the use of empirically proven theory as its basis. Unfortunately, the information systems researcher must either rely on the scant and poorly developed theory attributed to the field or borrow from theory developed for other fields of study, then endeavor to establish relevance in his own field. Consequently, the implication on practice is significant, as the discipline's body of knowledge continues to grow in a haphazard and uncertain manner that frequently fails to demonstrate practical relevance.

Innovation in Financial Services

Khoury, A. & Kellerman, B. (2010). Boundary pushers: as the global economy rebounds, the significance of technology and innovation for banks has never been greater. *Australian Banking & Finance* 2.8, 1.

This research details ways that banking institutions have begun to leverage new technology. Khoury and Kellerman surveyed banking industry executives and information technology professionals, asking questions about how technology is changing the way the industry conducts business. Each executive and IT professional quoted in the research discussed new technological innovations that their enterprise recently implemented or was considering.

Financial services executives, in conjunction with their respective IT professionals, represent the gatekeepers for new technology diffusion. Ultimately, the opinions, biases, and approachability of these key decision makers will determine not only what technology the enterprise will adopt, but how successful that implementation will be. The insights gained from the technological opinions of these executives, in their own words, represent a key component to identifying implementation challenges.

Measurement Instruments

Bagozzi, R. P., & Foxall, G. R. (1995). Construct validity and generalizability of the Kirton Adaption-Innovation inventory. *European Journal of Personality, 9*(3), 185-206.

The Kirton adaption-innovation (KAI) inventory instrument was previously developed to generally measure cognitive styles related to decision-making, creativity, and problem solving. The KAI has been used to measure factors that influence adoption behaviors for a variety of products; however, these researchers believed that the previous, uni-dimensional interpretation of the instrument was insufficient to capture the true characteristics of the innovator. The researchers sought to test the three-factor structure of the instrument using confirmatory factor analysis, using existing research as the theoretical basis, and to determine the degree of uniqueness of the three facets measured by the KAI. The researchers also sought to demonstrate the generalizability and adaptability of the KAI through the application of formal statistical tests.

The researchers administered the 32-item KAI to 305 managers and graduate management students and submitted the results for rigorous factor analysis. Results rejected the single-factor model in every case, supporting the researchers assertion that the KAI must be conceptualized using the three-factor model. Results supported a strong level of reliability, convergent and discriminant validity, and generalizability for the KAI across all samples.

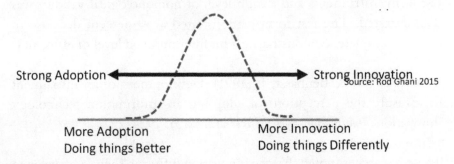

Source: Rod Ghani 2015

Strong Adoption ⟷ Strong Innovation

More Adoption
Doing things Better

More Innovation
Doing things Differently

Chin, W. W., Johnson, N., & Schwarz, A. (2008). A fast form approach to measuring technology acceptance and other constructs. *MIS Quarterly*, *32*(4), 687-703.

Chin et al examined the Technology Acceptance Model (TAM) developed by Davis (1989), citing the literature that has demonstrated the model's validity and reliability. Chin et al expressed reservations regarding the Likert scale method traditionally used with the TAM and sought instead to develop a more rapid, more efficient scale for measuring responses.

These researchers proposed the development of a fast form TAM instrument using a semantic differential scale. This scale, the researchers theorized, would not only provide a more expeditious way to collect data but would also allow future researchers to measure the attitude of respondents a more effective, cognitively based manner.

After converting the TAM to use a semantic differential response scale, Chin et al conducted surveys using the revised instrument and tested the results to assess the validity and reliability of the fast form through the survey of a group of university students. These 283 students were surveyed regarding their perceptions about a database technology application. Data was analyzed for efficiency of measure, and a comparison was done between the original and fast form TAM instruments. Analysis confirmed the psychometric equivalent between the original and the fast form instruments and a high level of nomonological validity was demonstrated. The fast form demonstrated a 40 percent decrease in time to complete, demonstrating a highly improved level of efficiency.

Moore, G. C., & Benbasat, I. (1991). Development of an instrument to measure the perceptions of adopting an information technology innovation. *Information Systems Research, 2*(3), 192-222.

These researchers noted that the innovation diffusion theories developed by Rogers (1995) were critical for research in the management information systems field, however existing research has produced no reliable instrument with which to measure adoption and diffusion of innovations within the enterprise. The researchers sought to develop a comprehensive instrument with which to conduct IT research, and to demonstrate the reliability and validity of the new instrument.

The researchers collected a large pool of items that had previously been used in the relevant research to measure innovation diffusion and also created new items for those areas in which they detected insufficient measurement. The stated objective of the researchers was to verify convergent and discriminant validity of the new scales through field tests and appropriate data analysis. Factor and discriminant analysis was used and the instrument was finalized with 38 items on eight scales designed to study initial adoption of innovation and the diffusion of the innovation.

Is Cloud Computing an Out-of-the-Box Solution?

Cloud computing platform pricing structures vary depending on the scope of the enterprise and its system architectural needs. Cloud computing deployment may present a more cost-effective solution for large-scale data management and analysis purposes than traditional platforms based on the wide flexibility available for cloud structure. This research cites a variety of commercial database application products and evaluates their overall performance when running cloud computing from data centers. The research further evaluates the overall ability of out-of-the-box software solutions to perform adequately in a cloud computing environment.

This research presents a focused analysis of one potential area of management resistance to technology, specifically the question of whether cloud computing requires custom created software solutions or if commercially available "out-of-the-box" software applications are able to meet the needs of the enterprise. Citing 36 distinct scholarly resources, Abadi provides a detailed examination of features that out-of-the-box software solutions should have, for the medium to large enterprise to achieve significant diffusion success with cloud computing architecture.

Bardhan, I.R., Demirkan, H., Kannan, P.K., Kauffman, R.J., & Sougastad, R. (2010). An interdisciplinary perspective on IT services management and service science. *Journal of Management Information Systems, 26*(4), 13.

This research addresses in depth the issues of information technology services, including cloud computing, from the basis of managerial and technical knowledge. The concept of service science is explored in depth from an interdisciplinary point of view. The roles of technology producers, consumers, integrators, consultants, user groups and regulators are examined in this context. The research proposes a variety of management practices that may improve information technology services within the enterprise.

Using over 200 scholarly resources, Bardhan et al examine the service science concept and how it applies specifically to the success of technology implementation. The research examines the role of cloud computing architecture from the complex perspective of services-oriented systems. The organizing principles of this management theory are applied to disruptive technologies and their implementation, and to management resistance in this scenario. Using a robust framework of analysis, Bardhan et al offer a variety of recommendations for paradigm shifts in management outlook, with regard to the diffusion of new and potentially disruptive technology.

ISACA. (2009). *Cloud Computing: Business benefits with security, governance and assurance perspectives.*

This white paper explores the growing pressure on enterprise to adopt innovative technology to meet the demands of the marketplace. Despite that pressure, the enterprise must be sensitive to concerns of data protection in the cloud environment. This paper details components of cloud computing, and examines potential risks versus benefits of cloud technology use.

ISACA is a non-affiliated, global think-tank providing knowledge certification, and education on information system security, governance, risks, and compliance. This paper represents an educational resource for enterprises that may be considering a cloud computing architecture implementation. The paper details a number of service and deployment models and the benefits and risks of each. This paper presents the data in a straightforward, unbiased manner and editorially encourages the development of industry standards and controls for cloud computing technology.

Jaeger, J. (2011, March). Cloud computing poses new risks, opportunities. *Compliance Week 86*(8), 1.

This research examines compliance concerns with regard to cloud computing technology. Jaeger cites several California compliance, audit, and information technology experts in their belief that cloud computing technology is intriguing but generally not considered safe by most experts in this specialty. Because the enterprise often does not maintain direct control of data in a cloud computing environment, that data is subject to compromise. Any such compromise renders the enterprise in non-compliance with a host of legal and governmental regulations and restrictions.

Jaeger devotes this research to relating the concerns of industry compliance professionals regarding cloud computing. Although this technology is the obvious future path of information technology solutions, this stakeholder group represents possibly the most adverse enterprise management sector. The resistance expressed by the attendees of this roundtable discussion is directly representative of the resistance factors found throughout the financial services industry.

Kim, W. (2009). Cloud computing: Today and tomorrow. *Journal of Object Technology, 1*(8), 65.

Kim proposed that cloud computing is in the early days of market adoption but that it is a significant trend that must be universally adopted by enterprise. The author details definitions and key terms related to cloud computing and further explores a number of adoption issues, offering a prognosis for the future of the cloud computing market.

Kim specifically details several technical issues that may impede the adoption of cloud computing on a general basis. These issues address a general platform of considerations with regard to cloud computing technology diffusion. Although Kim does not devote an extensive amount of information to specifics, this research presents an excellent overview of general considerations for adoption of cloud technology. In addition, the research cites a number of useful scholarly resources that may provide further data on this topic.

Weinhardt, C., Anandasivam, A., Blau, B., Borissov, N., Meinl, T., Michalk, W., & Stèoßer, J. (2009). Cloud computing – A classification, business models, and research directions. *Business & Information Systems Engineering, 1*(5), 391.

This research examines the specific details of the cloud computing paradigm including a detailed analysis of the characteristics of both cloud computing and the closely associated term of grid computing. This research distills several research projects relating to key concepts, pricing, and performance of cloud computing architecture and related issues. Weinhardt et al discuss business models that may be applied using existing cloud technology and the challenges that must be overcome.

Weinhardt et al cite 22 scholarly resources, including several significant research studies, in their analysis of cloud and grid computing. The authors, from the Institute of Information Systems and Management at Universitat Karlsruhe in Germany, offer insights into the existing research that other authors (particularly those from the United States) do not. While the technology and terminology does differ slightly in Europe, the overall structure of cloud computing is comparable. The sensibilities of United States technology experts differ somewhat from those of their European counterparts, and the insights offered here reflect a refreshing counterpoint.

Influencing Decision Factors to Adopt Cloud Computing

Research is considered generally to be the tool through which a science or discipline is informed and through which conceptual frameworks are developed (Gill & Bhattacherjee, 2009). Through empirical study, the researcher provides critical information to other researchers, to students and scholars, to those who practice in the field, and to society overall. The innovation diffusion theory model is used frequently in management information systems research, to help understand those factors that encourage, inhibit, or prevent the adoption of an artifact within a specific population (Fichman, 2004). Cloud computing, although considered to be "the next generation in computation" (Zamani, Akhtar, & Ahmad, 2011), has yet to receive any significant attention from information systems researchers, despite a proliferation of informational and analytical literature on the topic (Ahmed, Chowdhury, Ahmed, & Rafee, 2012). In order to establish a research framework to examine the diffusion of cloud computing within the financial services sector, it is necessary to examine other empirical studies related to the topic.

Researchers have explored the diffusion of cloud computing, albeit on a limited basis, in several industries. Low, Chen, and Wu (2011) explored factors leading to cloud computing adoption in Taiwan's high-tech sector. Low et al. sought to determine the extent that an organization's decision to adopt cloud technologies was influenced by eight specific variables (relative advantage, complexity, compatibility, top management support, firm size, technology readiness, competitive pressure, and trading partner pressure), incorporating technological, organizational, and environmental factors. For this study, the researchers surveyed managers of 500 randomly selected high-tech firms.

The researchers used a logistic regression technique with each of the eight variables to test the model, observing the high potential for multi-colinearity. They tested for reliability using Cronbach's alpha, and used factor analysis to evaluate construct validity. Logistic regression, goodness-of-fit, and p-value data demonstrated supporting evidence for five of the eight research hypotheses, demonstrating that perception of relative advantage, top management support, firm size, trading partner pressure, and competitive pressure all positively correlated to the adoption of cloud computing within the participating firms. Technological readiness, compatibility of the technology with company values/practices/needs, and complexity of the technology had no demonstrated effect. Low et al. (2011) stated that different factors are likely to influence the adoption of cloud computing in different industries and recommended future similar studies in less technologically focused sectors.

One such traditionally low-technology sector is the insurance sector. The significant financial, risk, and transfer-of-wealth implications of this sector have rendered insurance firms historically leery of unproven or radical technologies. Puelz (2010) explored the dichotomy between this inherent conservatism and the sector's need for an ever-increasing level of analytic and computational power. Puelz observed that the insurance sector has a well-defined business model and process structure, which may be melded together by technology in ways that greatly improve efficiency and viability. The research conducted by Puelz sought to identify insurers' perceived value of technology adoption, in this case the use of the internet and an electronic distribution channel ("online channel").

In this study, Puelz (2010) asked insurer members of two trade associations to rate the degree to which adoption of an electronic distribution channel reduced cost, enhanced revenue, and increased customer retention. Responses varied based on company size, with smaller companies placing greater emphasis on customer retention and larger companies seeking revenue enhancement. Virtually all of the participants in this study ranked internet technologies as either medium or high in influence on achieving these stated goals.

This research demonstrated the influence that technology has on the insurance sector, particularly in marketing, underwriting, and claims. Puelz (2010) stated that the adoption of emerging technology would separate "winners from losers" (p. 104) in the sector, going forward. Data from this study is displayed with statistical significance; however, Puelz did not state which statistical tests were used during analysis. Consequently, as statistical methods are unknown, it is impossible to verify reliability or validity. This research and its implications are critical to understanding the role that information systems place in the insurance sector today; consequently, it may be highly beneficial to see the results of similar studies that use a more significant number of participants, generally accepted analytical methods, and demonstrated, acceptable levels of construct validity and reliability.

Prior to the work done by Puelz (2010), Bradley and Stewart (2003) researched the proliferation of online banking in the financial services sector. The internet had become a significant technological factor for many industries; however, the banking sector took a conservative approach to adoption of this technology. The researchers sought to determine to what extent banks would consider the adoption of online banking and what factors were driving or inhibiting adoption. The research was designed using the theory of innovation diffusion but also considered factors of organizational aspiration.

The researchers in this study assembled a panel comprised of purposively sampled managers from retail banks, consultants, academicians, and experts in e-commerce and posed an online survey using closed- and open-ended questions. Using both qualitative and quantitative methods of data analysis, the researchers identified and categorized emergent themes and triangulated those with quantitative data. The results indicated that online banking diffused due to the technology's ability to reduce costs and facilitate customer interaction. Characteristics within the banking sector that encouraged adoption were increasing competition, the fact that other banks had adopted the technology, anticipated long-term consumer demand, and governmental influence. Sector inhibitors were a general lack of innovative culture in the sector and short-term consumer demand. Finally, inhibiting factors related to the technology itself were mainly issues of security followed by the difficulty in implementation due to legacy systems, a lack of available bandwidth, and the rapidity with which technology was evolving.

The research conducted by Bradley and Stewart (2003) indicated that online banking was considered at the time to be a radical innovation for the banking sector and that the technology caused a significant change in sector practices. Security concerns were the dominant inhibitor in the adoption of online banking, which is also a suspected reason that contemporary innovative technologies have not diffused in this sector at the same rate as in other industries. This research, using a mixed method approach, lacked some critical operational constructs and failed to acknowledge factors relating to validity. Nevertheless, the triangulation of qualitative and quantitative data increased validity levels to some degree.

The exploration of technology diffusion across industries presents several specific challenges to the researcher. Kerimoglu, Basoglu, and Daim (2008) explored the diffusion of enterprise resource planning (ERP) technologies by applying the technology acceptance model (TAM) considering also user satisfaction, user resistance, organizational memory, and environmental factors. The researchers hypothesized specifically that, among those participant firms who had adopted ERP, perceived usefulness, perceived ease of use, satisfaction, and various effects of the technology were influenced by factors related to the technology itself, organizational factors, user characteristics, and several factors related to project management. Using surveys obtained from sector-leading organizations and other SMEs across the electronics, white goods, agriculture, and energy industries, Kerimoglu et al. used measurement constructs based on prior research and several qualitative studies conducted by the researchers.

Kerimoglu et al. (2008) used reliability and factor analysis as well as Cronbach's alpha to establish validity in this research. Data were analyzed using paired *t*-tests, ANOVA, and linear regression analysis to address the relationship between the 15 hypotheses presented. The results demonstrated insights into those users who found the ERP technology to be useful and efficient, as well as the influence that technology and project management had on perceptions of organizational satisfaction with the technology. Participants who were satisfied attributed it to compatibility and flexibility in the technology.

Similar to the research conducted by Kerimoglu et al. (2008), Chao and Chandra (2012) sought to identify technology diffusion factors among small companies through the lens of strategic alignment factors. The researchers sought to understand how alignment is achieved based on characteristics of company owners or executive level decision-makers, particularly those relating to technology experience or expertise, perception, and vision. Chao and Chandra hypothesized that owner knowledge regarding information systems and technologies influenced organizational alignment with technology as well as the adoption of technology.

Chao and Chandra (2012) surveyed manufacturing and financial services organizations in three U.S. states. Regression analysis was used to analyze the data, with factor analyses and Cronbach's alpha calculations used to establish validity. Data analyses indicated that owner or decision-maker characteristics and knowledge correlated to the adoption of innovative technologies and perceived strategic alignment that resulted from technology adoption. Among the financial services firms that participated in the study, although the rate of adoption of traditional information systems technologies generally matched that of other industries, the adoption of innovative technologies lagged.

This research is significant because it is one of the few published studies evaluating the characteristics of decision-makers and the influence of those on the diffusion of innovative technology. The failure of an organization to adopt innovative technology may be correlated closely to low-level technical perceptions and sophistication level of decision-makers, hindering the ability of the organization to use innovative technology to support its business strategies and goals. Chao and Chandra (2012) called specifically for future research to examine the adoption of cloud computing models in relation to small business and strategic alignment factors.

Relevant literature and research has addressed factors of innovation diffusion, cloud computing, adopter characteristics, and the financial services and insurance sectors in the United States. Fichman (2004) stated that research in information systems innovation is critical as a driver of organizational competitiveness and is imperative based on the rapid advancement of innovative technologies. Current information systems research paradigms do not keep pace with the innovation-related needs of constituents, resulting in the need for a more aggressive and responsive set of research paradigms. Fichman described current paradigms of identifying and studying the ways and reasons that some firms possess the aptitude for innovation, essentially both the need for innovation and the ability to innovate successfully.

In the insurance sector, several factors contribute to the choice to adopt innovative technologies. Amirkhani, Salehahmadi, and Hajialiasgari (2011) explored the aspects of the insurance sector that affect innovation adoption decisions. Concerns about the nature of radical innovative technologies and their ability to prevail in the long term have caused this sector to lag frequently behind others in adoption. Amirkhani et al. examined the technology acceptance model (TAM) and its role in innovation diffusion in the insurance sector, including the application of both technological and behavioral factors to the analysis. The researchers stated that studies in this area historically used one or the other but rarely considered both.

Technology Diffusion

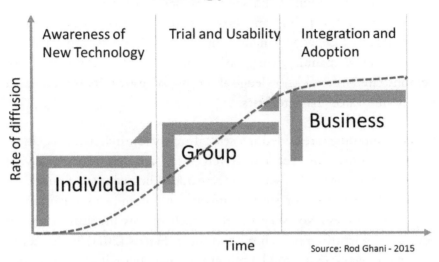

Source: Rod Ghani - 2015

A proliferation of analytical and informational research addressing cloud computing has emerged, which provides meta-analysis of current research and the gaps that exist in information systems. Ahmed et al. (2012) explored cloud computing specifically as it relates to contemporary information systems research, noting that this technology poses some of the greatest research challenges known today. Ahmed et al. recommended several critical courses for future research in this area, stating "there are still so many issues to be explored" (p. 207); however, no reference was made informing those who practice in the field. Zamani et al. (2011) also addressed research topics related to cloud computing and made recommendations for future study that considered the inherent challenges therein. Some of the challenges identified by these researchers did address technical issues and the importance of informing practice on reliability, liability, and security issues related to cloud computing.

Little research has explored the diffusion of information and knowledge management systems and artifacts in the insurance sector. Huang, Quaddus, Rowe, and Lai (2011) explored that dearth through extensive case study and analysis, including the development of a proposed research model. Huang et al. cited statistics supporting their assertion that the insurance sector plays a significant and critical role in society due to the amount of money and social responsibility regularly entrusted to insurers by the public and other businesses. Compared to other industries using knowledge management technologies (pharmaceutical, biotechnology, manufacturing, and high-tech), the insurance sector demonstrated inferior knowledge about available artifacts and a distinct lack of innovator characteristics.

Cloud computing is regarded as a critical area of research in management information systems, yet a relatively small amount of the relevant literature is comprised of scientific research. The majority of published research is analytical or simply informative, despite its inclusion in respected sources. Not surprisingly, much of this literature calls for additional scientific research on this topic. Harris (2011) wrote about the many ways that cloud computing may benefit the insurance sector, citing statistics from studies conducted by solution providers and trade associations; however this data serves little purpose beyond providing guidance for scientific research. Kenealy (2011) stressed the need for all insurers to move toward adopting cloud computing but cited a lack of sector and governmental standards addressing cloud technologies as a major inhibitor to cloud adoption in the insurance sector. Unfortunately, Kenealy provided no empirical or scientific support for these assertions. Ruquet (2011) listed risks inherent in the adoption of cloud computing for insurance agencies. Ruquet's research, published in an established trade publication, sought to advise insurance organizations on a critical aspect of practice, based solely on quotes obtained from a technology vice president from Travelers Insurance. McAfee (2011), a research scientist from the Massachusetts Institute of Technology, made significant recommendations for the adoption of cloud computing based on statistics from an IBM study and information provided by Microsoft.

Gill and Bhattacherjee (2009) stated that management information systems researchers faced significant challenges, to the extent that the very future of the discipline may be threatened. Gill and Bhattacherjee stated that the other challenge faced by information systems researchers is that their ability to inform external customers, including students, practitioners, and interrelated disciplines, has actually begun to decline. The barriers cited here are mirrored by many academicians and subject matter experts: Researchers are failing to inform practice by focusing too much on a level of theoretical advancement that practitioners either do not understand or do not believe applies to practice; dissemination of relevant research is failing because distribution channels used for its publication do not reach those practitioners who most need the information; and, most importantly, the very paradigms upon which information systems research field has been built are not effective for informing practice in the sector.

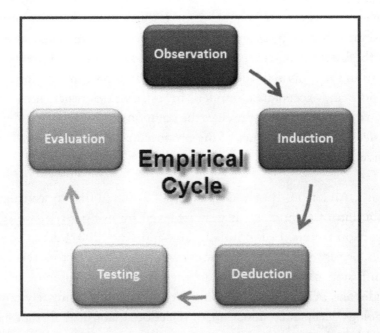

Empirical evidence exists to support research in the diffusion of information systems innovation, in the information systems artifact of cloud computing, in technology diffusion among small businesses and in the insurance portion of the financial services sector, and in the role that personal characteristics of company owners or executive decision-makers play in enterprise innovation. In the proposed study, the researcher seeks to combine these elements to meet a critical need in the knowledge base, through the conduct of a study into the diffusion of cloud computing technology among small- and medium-sized insurers in the United States. The empirical basis for the proposed study is the theory of innovation diffusion, based on contemporary interpretations that apply the technology acceptance model. The purpose of this research is to identify and interpret those factors that influence the behavior of insurance executives when choosing to adopt or reject cloud computing technology in the enterprise, and the individual adaptive-innovative traits and characteristics of the decision-maker himself.

Inadequate theory development and measurement constructs are common challenges in information systems research (Moore & Benbasat, 1991). To overcome these challenges, prior research addressing innovation diffusion, technology acceptance models, and adopter characteristics form the basis for research constructs, measurement instruments, and analysis in the proposed study. Existing research measuring innovation diffusion and acceptance models in relation to other innovative information technologies provides the components necessary to identify and measure each construct of the proposed research individually and in correlation.

Howard, Anderson, Busch, & Nafus (2009) stated that measuring the distribution of technology is best achieved by using a relevant set of comparison factors. Liang, Nilesh, Hu, and Xue (2007) demonstrated that enterprise owners or decision-makers mediate factors related to the diffusion of an innovation in the enterprise. Consequently, the attitudes and belief systems of these decision-makers ultimately govern technology acceptance, adoption, or rejection. Liang et al. further stated that, although external forces may exert pressure on adoption models, external forces do not affect the behavior of the organization without first influencing agents of change. Based on these factors, the researcher proposes to study those factors that influence the characteristics, beliefs, and behaviors of executive decision-makers.

Melville and Ramirez (2008) stated that the analysis of the characteristics identified by Rogers is a necessary inclusion in innovation diffusion research; however, an examination of these characteristics alone is insufficient. Davis (1989) developed a basis for both perceived ease of use and perceived usefulness of innovative technology through his development of the technology acceptance model (TAM). Chin, Johnson, and Schwarz (2008) built on Davis's research of the TAM, noting that research relevant to the TAM has verified the relevance of these characteristics for the study of innovation diffusion.

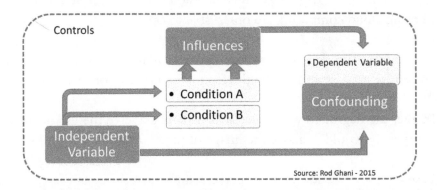

Although the variables identified by Rogers (2003) and Davis (1989) are highly relevant to the proposed research, the study design must also include an exploration of those characteristics inherent in the decision-maker himself. Bagozzi and Foxall (1995) examined the location of individuals on an adaptiveness-innovativeness scale and its relationship to differences in the cognitive style of decision-makers. This measurement has been used in a variety of relevant applications, including the evaluation of computer technology adoption.

Dependent and Independent Variables

Voluntariness of Use, the degree to which decision makers perceive the use of cloud computing as voluntary.

Relative Advantage, the degree to which decision makers perceive the use of cloud computing as better than alternatives.

Compatibility, the degree to which decision makers perceive the use of cloud computing as consistent with existing values, needs, and past experiences.

Complexity, the degree to which decision makers perceive the use of cloud computing as being difficult to use.

Observability, the degree to which decision makers perceive the results of using cloud computing are observable to others.

Trialability, the degree to which decision makers perceive that the enterprise may experiment with cloud computing prior to adoption;

Image, the degree to which decision makers perceive the use of cloud computing would enhance the image of the enterprise.

Ease of Use, decision makers' perceived characteristics of the ease of use cloud computing.

Usefulness, decision makers' perceived characteristics of the usefulness cloud computing.

Relative Cost, decision makers' perceived cost attributes of cloud computing.

Security, decision makers' perceived security attributes of cloud computing; and Innovativeness, decision makers' personal characteristics of adaptiveness-innovation.

The dependent variable for the project is the adoption or rejection of cloud computing in the enterprise.

Carlo, Lyytinen, and Rose (2011) stated that using variables to control for organizational size and other enterprise-specific factors that may influence the adoption of innovation is critical. Certain organizational characteristics may better position the enterprise to adopt innovative, radical, or disruptive technology; and the researcher must exercise great care to identify other factors that may influence adopter behavior. Through the course of the proposed project, the researcher will collect a variety of control variables regarding the participants, including title or organizational role, age, gender, and time in current position. In addition, information will be collected regarding the participant's organization, including lines of business written, annual premium collected, public or private company, and enterprise geographic location. Although some of these control variables may not affect the decision to adopt cloud technology, each will be analyzed through factor analysis to identify which should be used in the main analysis of data.

Research Survey Sample

The research project surveyed chief executives of U.S. insurance and financial companies regarding their company's adoption of cloud computing technologies. This population consists of United States insurance carriers engaged in property and casualty insurance, life insurance and benefits, or a combination of those lines of business. From this population, approximately 650 companies randomly selected to participate in the survey. To achieve a power level of 0.8 and an effect size of 0.3, a power analysis calculation specified a sample size of approximately 200. In anticipation of a 45 percent response rate from those companies sampled, sufficient data was collected so that approximately 35 percent of the responses were used to conduct factor analyses to identify factors that significantly influence the decision to adopt cloud technology, as well as to demonstrate research validity.

The sampling method study consisted of surveying the chief executive or decision-maker of each firm. The survey items for the proposed study was based on the demonstrated research of Moore and Benbasat (1991), Chin, Johnson, and Schwarz (2008), and Bagozzi and Foxall (1995). These researchers demonstrated the reliability and validity of their respective research instruments for measuring characteristics of decision makers regarding innovation diffusion and technology acceptance, how those influence the diffusion of innovation in the enterprise, and the personal psychometric characteristics of high-level decision makers. In addition to the survey items designed to measure innovative technology adoption characteristics, the researcher shall collect a variety of moderating and control variables regarding the company and the executive personally, as described above.

Measurement

The measurement instruments for the subject study have been selected based on significant support of each in the literature and the demonstrated reliability, validity, and generalizability of each. The primary goal of Moore and Benbasat (1991) in developing their measurement instrument was to provide future innovation diffusion researchers with demonstrated reliability and validity of measurement. Moore and Benbasat stated that reliability levels may vary depending on the purpose of the research, and the researcher should consider any additional factors; however, the instrument should provide a useful tool with which to study the diffusion and adoption of innovative technologies in the proposed study.

Data Analysis

Reliability and validity are critical characteristics of research to demonstrate the ability to repeat the test over time with a comparable degree of accuracy, to demonstrate the adequacy of research methods, and to verify the veracity of results. In the research of Moore and Benbasat (1991), Chin et al. (2008), and Bagozzi and Foxall (1995), validity and reliability were demonstrated through a variety of relevant data and factor analyses, including the use of Cronbach's alpha. In each case, a high degree of reliability and validity was demonstrated for each aspect of the research. To determine what if any effect the independent/control variables have on whether or not the enterprise adopts cloud computing technologies will be determined using a two-tailed analysis of variance (ANOVA).

The available cloud computing literature is largely informational and opinion-based, lacking significant empirical or scientific support. Those who perform scientific research on the diffusion of cloud computing have universally concluded that there is a pressing need for research in this area. Many researchers have proposed study models to explore these subjects; however, if researchers are using the proposed models, the results remain largely unreported in scientific journals. Gill and Bhattacherjee (2009) stated that, even when relevant scientific research is conducted, it often fails to inform practice or even reach practitioners at all.

The proposed research project will provide critical information to inform the management information systems discipline and the insurance sector regarding the influence that executive-level decision makers have on the adoption of innovative technology. This research has the potential to advance innovation diffusion and technology acceptance theory to consider the influence that decision-maker characteristics, perceptions, and belief systems have on technology adoption. This complements prior research that has considered characteristics of the innovative technology itself or of the organization. Results may inform information systems practice in several relevant ways and allow the insurance sector to gain valuable insight into using innovative technologies to gain competitive advantage in a challenging market economy.

A practical examination of sector needs calls for one approach but the advancement of theoretical knowledge warrants a different approach. To fulfill the obligations of the dissertation, the student researcher must demonstrate theoretical development or enrichment. If the student can contribute to theory while also developing information that can somehow benefit the sector in some practical way, he might help bridge the research-practice gap. The goal of theory-based research that is adaptable to praxis must be one that is adopted universally in the sector, if it is to grow and thrive in the future. The proposed project is an example that illustrates one approach the researcher may use when endeavoring to meet the underlying imperatives of research while also providing practical benefit to the sector he serves.

The researcher provides critical information to others through the responsible conduct and dissemination of empirical study. Through research, relevant theory is advanced, knowledge is created, and practice is informed. In the research process, the researcher must rely on empirical studies and must possess the ability to understand research methods and analyses as well as to assess critically the meaning and relevance of results. The researcher must identify critical gaps in existing research and design meaningful studies to advance theory and discipline-related knowledge to address those divergences. Current information systems research has generally failed to address innovation diffusion and the adoption of the cloud computing paradigm in the financial services sector, although this area of practice should be further informed. The researcher must strive to meet the practical needs of his field; however, he must meet this imperative only through the use of a responsible, scientific, and theory-based approach.

PART III

Case Study I

User Satisfaction Experience

The degree to which an end user is satisfied with a technology solution depends on a variety of determinants. Larsen (2009) researched these determinants, which include effective communications and user training efficacy. These satisfactions, whether positive or negative, will "form a systematic pattern... negatively or positively across determinants of satisfaction" (Larsen, 2009, p. 659). Critical implementation aspects, for example ensuring that enterprise business objectives for implementation are communicated to users at all levels, are likely not intuitive to the implementing organization. These and other imperatives should most appropriately be tasked to implementation partners in many enterprise network installations, establishing the basis, along with the service-level agreement itself, for the ensemble implementation paradigm presented by Xue, Liang, Boulton, and Snyder (2005).

Xue et al (2005) examined the interaction dynamics between people and technology. With specific regard to enterprise resource networks, the ensemble view of this relationship as described by Xue et al resembles the theories proposed by Goo and Huang (2008). ERP systems, although traditionally regarded as technology solutions, are designed, implemented, and operated by people. Moreover, these systems are designed to directly replicate those actions and thought processes traditionally undertaken by people. As such, they must be regarded as a critical part of the social structure of the enterprise. Unless such resource networks are designed and implemented with the culture and needs of the people, the necessary relationships are unlikely to develop. This may easily result in the regarded failure of implementation.

Case Study II

Vendor Relationships

Just as the relationship must be cultivated between the enterprise and the enterprise resource network, successful resource network implementation depends on having all of the critical factors of the vendor relationship in place. Krigsman (2010a) explored the SLA that California's Marin County executed with Deloitte Consulting for the implementation of an enterprise resource network. The relationship between Marin and Deloitte deteriorated sharply over time, resulting in a communications failure and ultimately a failure of the technology solution. Krigsman expressed the opinion that Marin was largely at fault for the failure, stating that the country's management and staff were unable to handle the significant operational transformation that a wide-scale ERP implementation brought about and that Marin displayed a lack of communication skill and organizational maturity. Marin's documents and status reports indicate that the municipality, in hindsight, believed it had relied too much on Deloitte and felt that the consultant was not as interested in a positive outcome as was Marin County.

Krigsman (2010b) explored a similar failure at Lumber Liquidators, where poor user training was blamed. The company blamed an enterprise network implementation for its ongoing failure in 2010 to meet customer orders. Consequently, the company posted significant financial losses. The company previously used legacy systems that include Excel spreadsheets to run a retail operation with 225 stores and $650 million in annual revenue (Krigsman, 2010b). The implementation of a comprehensive networked solution was a major shock to the company that no one prepared them for. Their service and implementation partner, a company called DataXstream, insufficiently prepared the company for the technical, social, and cultural changes that the implementation would bring about. Krigsman observed that the blame for the system failure was split between poorly trained consultant personnel, high consultant personnel turnover, poor vendor selection and bad vendor management on the part of Lumber Liquidators.

In the cases of both Marin County, California, and Lumber Liquidators, costly failures occurred as the apparent result of poor commitment and trust within the service-level agreements between the companies and their technology partners. Certainly it is also possible that in one or both cases, the wrong vendor or implementation partner was selected, although neither blamed the ERP application itself. Blackwell, Shehab, and Kay (2006) attributed this type of misstep to the fact that many companies, depending on the industry, lack the type of in-house technical management personnel who can make wise and informed decisions when selecting technical partners. In addition, insufficient or uninformed technical managers may be unaware of the social and cultural implications of major-scale implementations. Although the enterprise may hope that their selected technology or implementation partner will adequately communicate all the potential risks and benefits, it cannot be assumed. Blackwell, Shehab, and Kay cautioned that the implementation must be considered primarily from an organizational and operational viewpoint, not as simply the installation of a new technology system.

Service-Level Agreement Success Factors

Benaroch, Dai, and Kauffman (2010) explored the factors that contract flexibility in service-level agreements must consider, including pricing methods and claims analysis strategies. These and other influential factors are critical for inclusion when entering into service-level agreements with technology partners. One key factor, volatility of demand, drives the need for technological outsourcing in many enterprises. SLAs must consider demand fluctuation as an influential factor, as enterprise demand as well as global economic fluctuation may reduce the prevailing service unit cost, leading the enterprise to question the vendor about cost reduction. Alternately, if service unit costs increase, the vendor may exert resistance toward the enterprise or become less responsive than to other clients. Benaroch et al described a new approach to contract construction to address these factors, including fixed subscription fee pricing, which will help reduce the high cost to the enterprise that results from vendor switching.

Sen, Raghu, and Vinze (2010) also addressed demand variation in service-level agreements, but emphasized the importance of also incorporating user preference considerations. The importance of including information-sharing provisions increased the stability of SLAs and significantly improved collaboration between the enterprise and the service provider in these case studies. Although variation in demand volume is of critical concern, the variation of user preference significantly increases the complexity of the service environment. Nonhomogeneous demand patterns may be addressed in the SLA by using a dynamic pricing approach incorporating volume-price adjustment strategies or by using a priority pricing approach incorporating a user-defined service urgency. Either way, resources must be appropriately allocated though a combination of price consideration and resource level adjustment.

Additional influence factors to be considered in SLA performance are communication and feedback standards, conflict arbitration, and specific enforcement of terms (Goo, Kishore, Rao, & Nam, 2009). Goo et al identified three types of SLA terms, foundational, change, and governance, and stressed the importance of enterprise consideration of factors that comprise each category. If these provisions are adhered to by the organization when implementing a broad-scope SLA, establish critical contingencies for dealing with future areas of concern that may arise. Desired outcomes may be more easily achieved and the rapid evolution of technologies and business conditions will be less likely to interfere with the execution of the agreement.

Conclusion

Service-level agreements, beyond the obvious standards of definition and terms, encompass a variety of uncertain and unstructured conditions. Vendor relationships, traditionally managed through the identification of terms, performance measurement instruments, and penalties or rewards based on performance, are actually far more complex than these basic standards could address. The vendor relationship ideally generates benefit for the enterprise and its stakeholders, although some levels of benefit are difficult to measure unless a critical failure happens, as demonstrated in the implementation case studies discussed above. When the enterprise has significant investment in the vendor relationship, the agreements that govern that relationship must consider those factors that encourage an ongoing productive and mutually beneficial relationship between the parties.

References

Benaroch, M., Dai, Q., & Kauffman, R. J. (2010). Should we go our own way? Backsourcing flexibility in IT services contracts. *Journal of Management Information Systems, 26*(4), 317-358.

Blackwell, P., Shehab, E. M., & Kay, J. M. (2006). An effective decision-support framework for implementing enterprise information systems within SMEs. *International Journal of Production Research, 44*(17), 3533-3552.

Goo, J., & Huang, C. D. (2008). Facilitating relational governance through service level agreements in IT outsourcing: An application of the commitment–trust theory. *Decision Support Systems, 46* (1), 216-232.

Goo, J., Kishore, R., Rao, H. R., & Nam, K. (2009). The role of service level agreements in relational management of information technology outsourcing: An empirical study. *MIS Quarterly, 33*(1), 119-145.

Kauffman, R. J., & Tsai, J. Y. (2009). The Unified Procurement Strategy for Enterprise Software: A Test of the "Move to the Middle" Hypothesis. *Journal of Management Information Systems, 26*(2), 177-204.

Krigsman, M. (2010, September). Understanding Marin County's $30 million ERP failure. *IT Project Failures, CNET.*

Krigsman, M. (2010, November). Understanding Lumber Liquidators' ERP failure. *IT Project Failures, CNET.*

Larsen, T. J. (2009). A multilevel explanation of end–user computing satisfaction with an enterprise resource planning system within an international manufacturing organization. *Computers in Industry, 60* (9), 657–668.

Sen, S., Raghu, T. S., & Vinze, A. (2010). Demand information sharing in heterogeneous IT services environments. *Journal of Management Information Systems, 26*(4), 287–316.

Xue, Y., Liang, H., Boulton, W. R., & Snyder, C. A. (2005). ERP implementation failures in China: Case studies with implications for ERP vendors. *International Journal of Production Economics, 97* (3), 279–295.

Case Study III

Building Information Modeling for the Construction Enterprise

Man has constructed buildings throughout documented history. Few modern technological advances apply to construction however, and many building methods remain unchanged from centuries ago. Modern construction enterprises must rely on technology to assist with the planning of stages of building projects. Even though manufacturing and other industries have used three-dimensional modeling technology for decades, the construction industry had only two-dimensional computer aided design and drafting (CAD) to assist with project design until recently (Sanders, 2010). Although CAD technologies represented a dramatic improvement over hand drafting, this tool solved only a portion of the problems associated with planning large construction projects. The advent of Building Information Modeling (BIM) technologies will greatly assist the building industry into the modern technological age.

Construction material costs have escalated drastically as a result of material shortages and economic conditions. Many companies have scaled back their workforce because of shrinking profit margins and a lack of projects (Gonchar, 2009). Construction enterprises must seek ways to carry their workload with less personnel and higher direct costs. These companies must be able to achieve a specific level of profitability on construction projects. BIM technology helps builders achieve those goals in many ways.

Essentially, BIM technology allows architects, engineers, and contractors to virtually design, schedule, and construct a building project in a three-dimensional format (Sanders, 2010). That ability provides a number of significant procedural advantages, drastically improving the contractor's ability to complete the project in a shorter time and – ideally – with a lower cost. A BIM project model involves a great deal more than a simple three-dimensional rendering of the planned building.

BIM provides every detail of the project, down to the location of the drywall screws (Sanders, 2010). Project plans are no longer the primary tool for building a project; rather they are simply a report printed from the project database (Post, 2008). A project virtualized in the BIM environment can generate simulations of project phases and individual components. These capabilities "minimize the chances for error and reduce the cost of the project" (O'Brien, 2010, p. 33). Combined with Global Positional System (GPS) applications and topographical mapping, BIM can render the building directly onto the specific construction site.

In many construction scenarios, companies must construct the same building in multiple locations. CAD technology required entirely new project plans for each site, even if the structure were the same as a previous one. In the BIM environment, designers can cut and paste elements from one project to another, drastically reducing the architectural timeline (Gonchar, 2009). The construction enterprise can share a project's digital model with other team members anywhere in the world. Team members in different countries can conduct a virtual walk-through of the project together, reviewing design elements and logistics (Gonchar, 2009).

Another significant advantage to using BIM systems involves the warranty and maintenance processes. The contractor can turn the virtual model over to the property managers and engineers responsible for maintaining the facility and those teams can use the model to troubleshoot system failures. Should the project owner desire to modify or expand the building in the future, the building model serves as full construction "as-built" documents, demonstrating exactly how each component was designed and constructed (O'Brien, 2010). In this way, the power of BIM extends substantially past the design phase of a project.

As with any new technology, the enterprise can expect to encounter some challenges with implementation. BIM instantly changes the very workflow and organization of a construction project (Post, 2008). Builders can expect to have every organization process affected.

Companies must anticipate this impact because field activities must mesh with office processes and financial implications must be closely monitored. Profit is in the details and the enterprise must monitor those details when implementing such a significant process (Johansmeyer, 2008).

Aside from direct cost and the overhead involved to implement BIM technology, the construction enterprise may encounter the most significant hurdle to implantation from company personnel. Other companies who have implemented the technology "report that they are still grappling with BIM technology and 'sociology'" (Post, 2008, p. 2). Some experts recommend an incremental roll-out of any BIM system, allowing everyone to become accustomed to working in the environment prior to applying the technology to real-world construction projects. BIM technology promises to change every aspect of the construction industry, and "construction doesn't change easily" (O'Brien, 2010, p. 34).

The cost of purchasing and implementing BIM is the most significant consideration for the construction enterprise. The hardware and software required is at least twice the cost of the equivalent CAD equipment (Post, 2008). Full BIM rollouts can take months or even years to successfully accomplish. In addition, many municipalities are currently unable to accept construction documents created with BIM for the purposes of permitting (Post, 2008). Despite these concerns, BIM technology is becoming the state-of-the-art method of producing construction documentation. Fortunately, most firms who have adopted the technology believe it was worth the cost and effort involved. The majority of construction enterprises using a BIM system report a favorable Return on Investment (ROI) (Sanders, 2010).

One of the significant reasons cited by current users for increased financial performance is the substantial ability BIM provides for the coordination of building trade contractors. In traditional project plans, designers documented each major trade's work on a separate page of the plans. Trade conflicts were commonplace with two-dimensional project plans. Architects and engineers inadvertently placed structural steel members in the way of HVAC ducting or water lines. Often these conflicts would go unnoticed until workers detected the conflict during construction, long after contractors had fabricated materials and incurred those costs.

BIM eliminates virtually all such conflicts, potentially saving wasted material costs and cutting substantial time off the construction schedule (Sanders, 2010). Trade coordination that previously took "months and months and months" (O'Brien, 2010, p. 37) can now be completed in a very small fraction of that time. As contractors typically are fined for going past their deadline, and often incentivized for accelerating the project schedule, this feature alone may provide positive financial returns.

In this age of environmental consciousness, BIM offers several "green" technology features that construction enterprises may find desirable. BIM project models provide detailed data regarding building energy profiles and sustainable design. The project team can modify various structural elements easily to increase energy performance (Sanders, 2010). This ability offers the building owner potential energy cost savings in addition to demonstrating a high level of corporate social responsibility.

BIM technology is still in its infancy. The first-generation virtual modeling technology is still expensive to purchase and implement, particularly for small and medium-sized enterprises (SMEs). Most experts agree, however, that very few significant construction projects will be built without it, even within five to 10 years (O'Brien, 2010). Even if they do not intend to implement BIM immediately, contracting enterprises must develop a comprehensive project deployment plan that incorporates future adoption of this critical technology.

Case Study IV

Micro Enterprises

Business enterprises, to compete in today's dynamic and volatile economic conditions, must cultivate knowledge, display expertise, and deliver significant value in a variety of specialized environments (Bannock, 2005). For many business owners however, internal corporate resources may be insufficient or periodically unavailable to meet these emerging demands. As the requirements of business success become more dependent on specialization, the business owner may find it impossible to successfully maintain the pace of knowledge development required to support decisions and enterprise growth (Pearson, 2011). Business owners may find tremendous benefit in the outsourcing of some aspects of knowledge creation, especially for the purpose of decision support. Through consultation with a variety of diverse knowledge suppliers, the enterprise may successfully establish a network of resources that will enable it to thrive in the marketplace.

Business owners, particularly those with micro or small enterprise companies, face a variety of challenges not present for larger, resource-rich business enterprises. Bannock (2005) observed that the concept of small business is not clearly defined but rather a relative concept. Small business enterprises are both desirable and vulnerable, because they encourage a competitive business climate yet their success is often subject to the whims of that same economic culture. Small businesses offer a means for the individual to become autonomous from the corporate culture and ideally to create wealth, independence, and self-expression. Unfortunately, few small and medium business enterprises have access to capital markets, overdraft protection, or term loans, resulting in a high degree of financial disadvantage compared to large corporations. Salles (2006) defined several characteristics of small business enterprises, identifying these companies as a "major part of the productive system, and its main factor for renewal" (p. 229). Where large companies exist typically to satisfy an identified need or demand, small business enterprises work to both satisfy those same needs and to discover new needs or demands that may also exist in the marketplace.

Small companies often make decisions quickly and informally, while large businesses must adhere to formal decision-making policies and procedures. The decision-makers within small companies typically make decisions on a wide variety of levels with many implications, whereas those individuals within large companies are frequently limited in scope and influence in their decisions. Problem solving within big business often occurs in a predetermined manner, but small business enterprises possess the flexibility to approach problems in novel and dynamic ways. Finally, with regard to the overall procedural approach, small business enterprises use less formalized procedure and have the ability to dynamically modify policy as needed, whereas large business enterprises must typically adhere to formal policies already in place or face an arduous route to modifying those procedures.

Based on these characteristics, the decision-making process within small business enterprises differs significantly from how decisions are made in a large company environment. Pearson (2009) warned that small businesses may mistakenly believe that formal or structured processes have no purpose in the organization, when these businesses may indeed have the greatest need for specialized decision or procedural support. The best small business decision-makers recognize the limitations of their company and do not seek to be experts in every aspect of business operations. Owners of small companies are best served by creating and nurturing opportunities to grow the company, rather than becoming mired exclusively in rote operational tasks. Consequently, owners of small businesses often seek experts or business consultants to provide marketplace advantages and assist in the knowledge creation or identification to support decision making.

Engaging the services of other business enterprises to assist in operational improvement frequently leads to value creation for the organization (Pearson, 2009). Expert consultants create value for small business enterprises through the contribution and application of knowledge, assets, and techniques to improve operational performance. Implementing business solutions and applying contributed knowledge will allow the small business enterprise owners and decision makers to make judgments, internally and externally, leading to effective and rapid decisions (Hall & Paradice, 2005).

Choosing the right contributors for the small business enterprise decision support system involves many complex considerations. Araz and Ozkarahan (2007) posited that, in today's economic climate, such choices must not be made solely on the classic criteria of cost, quality, and delivery. Rather the small business owner must use practices of strategic sourcing, wherein many other criteria are considered, including level of technology and innovativeness, cooperative attitude, cost-reduction capabilities, and quality management practices.

Clark, Jones, and Armstrong (2007) described the process of constructing management support systems (MSS) for the purpose of decision support within the enterprise. Decision support systems (DSS) leverage evolving technology, help reduce the level of uncertainty often inherent in the decision-making process, and generally support the decision-maker efficiently and effectively. Salles (2006) described the way that systems theory may provide a framework to assist the small business enterprise owner in determining the components necessary to construct the DSS. Those decision systems that evolve appropriately will remain stable and endow stability to the operational environment.

The challenge for the small business owner in developing decision support systems is that he may lack formal understanding of knowledge-based systems and, as a result, haphazardly pursue the compilation of data and its application to enterprise challenges (Bannock, 2005). An appreciation of the importance of decision support systems, combined with a solid of understanding of how these valuable tools function and assist the enterprise, will allow the business owner to apply the methods and best practices of DSS to the organization effectively. To accomplish this, the owner or decision-maker must develop an understanding of decision support concepts, then identify and define the specific decision support needs of the organization (Duan & Xu, 2005).

Power (2002) developed a taxonomy for classification of decision support systems, categorizing the concept as communications-driven, data-driven, document-driven, knowledge-driven, or model-driven. The small business enterprise owner or decision-maker might certainly wish to develop systems to encompass some or all of these categories, to create an enterprise-wide solution to problem-solving, knowledge creation, and decision-making. Knowledge management and decision support systems may work well together to create symbiotic management tools for the small business (Kesner, 2010).

Duan and Xu (2005) identified the components of a decision support system, which are the knowledge or data, the model by which the information will be evaluated and applied, the method by which the user accesses and evaluates the information, and the user himself. The central component to the success of a DSS is the models and analytical methods by which the knowledge will be applied. Decision support systems must not be expected to replace the owner's decision-making, but instead to improve its effectiveness.

Traditional decision support systems were generally closed, passive systems, wherein decision makers scanned data in search of discrepancies, ran ad hoc queries, and arrived at conclusions. Adla, Laskri, and Soubie (2007) proposed that an intelligent decision support system (IDSS) may expand those traditional paradigms and add expert knowledge and collaboration technologies to enhance decision support in the small business enterprise. Bannock (2005) noted a common tendency to apply knowledge and experience gained from large business enterprises to small businesses. Decision support systems developed for and used in small company environments must recognize the specific needs of the small business (Duan & Xu, 2005).

Upon establishing the specific needs of the organization, the small business enterprise owner must determine what type of decision support system will best address those needs. In the past, many business and economic theorists regard DSS as a purely mechanical process, often in the form of computer-based applications. Contemporary researchers have determined however that decisions support systems may assume a variety of forms, including educational programs and consultants in addition to a wide variety of sophisticated computer applications and technologies (Pearson, 2009).

Computer-based DSS, although not the main focus of this analysis, does merit some mention. Duan and Xu (2005) identified four types of computing technology DSS applications, including out-of-the-box software packages, custom designed software programs commissioned by the company, software written or designed in-house, and computer applications customized or designed by the owner or decision-maker himself. Little research exists on the latter two categories; however research has demonstrated that commercial and bespoke software DSS applications are effective in assisting small business enterprises in making business decisions (Bannock, 2005).

Knowledge in the form of digital data may be well utilized by the enterprise for decision-making support, however this option is only one of the many potential tools available to the small business enterprise owner or decision-maker. Adla, Laskri, and Soubie (2007) suggested that decision support systems should be used in a wide variety of contexts and encompass "all aspects related to supporting people in making decisions" (p. 293). Hall and Paradice (2005) explored the various methods of decision support, including artificial intelligence, organizational learning, computer information systems, and expert systems. Decision support through expert systems allows the organization to become more successfully influenced by communication, learning, and inquiry (Clark, Jones, & Armstrong, 2007) and incorporates demonstrated humanistic principles of knowledge management into the decision-making process (Kesner, 2010).

As noted, small business owners must seek out the services of experts and a variety of business consultants because the innate structure of the small business typically precludes the company from having the resources to employ experts in every necessary discipline. The owner or decision maker then becomes, in a way, the director of several smaller business concerns as he coordinates and manages these experts and consultants. Ehmke, Akridge, Lusk, and Lusk (2004) noted that consultants assist small business owners by adding an outside perspective and contributing a variety of specialized skills, filling in gaps within the company's own staff. Similar to internal hiring practices, the enterprise owner must exercise care and diligence in identifying, evaluating, selecting, and managing experts and consultants, to achieve the greatest benefit.

Using best practices for choosing knowledge vendors will allow the business owner to achieve the greatest benefit from the relationship. Ehmke, Akridge, Lusk, and Lusk (2004) suggested that the decision-maker begin with a thorough understanding of the project or subject for which the vendor will be selected, to allow the expert to provide the best results. Defining the project scope in writing will allow both sides to be clear about objectives. Barley and Kunda (2006) warned that, although consultancy and outsourcing have become representative of a new way of conducting business, these topics remain significantly misunderstood. Contract knowledge providers comprise what these researchers termed a new itinerant type of workforce, injecting a new and beneficial professional dynamic.

For the outsourcing of knowledge creation decision support to achieve maximum efficacy, the small business enterprise owner must understand the theories of consultancy from the contractor's perspective. Those people who offer their services in this way have, much like the entrepreneurs who engage their services, "rejected the familiar pains and comforts of organizational life for the freedom and accompanying risks of the marketplace" (Barley & Kunda, 2006, p. 45). Desouza and Awazu (2006) referred to this new class of consultants as Contingent Knowledge Workers, identifying their differences from the traditional contingent workforce of seasonal or project laborers. Contingent Knowledge Workers contribute all of the benefits and flexibility detailed above while contributing knowledge that has been applied and tested in a variety of situations and environments. The organization is not required to invest the time and capital normally required to produce such sophisticated knowledge; it is instead available quickly, in exchange only for a reasonable fee.

The management of contingent knowledge workers, consultants, and other external experts may threaten to overwhelm the small business owner unless a strategic plan is implemented to assist his coordination efforts. Issues of information security, confidentiality, and integrity must remain foremost in the business owner's mind, along with matters of ethics, corporate social responsibility, and stakeholder obligation. Aside from these critical considerations, the business owner must understand the specific challenges inherent to the shifting boundaries of consultants and external experts. According to Desouza, and Awazu (2006), issues of knowledge hostility may threaten the relationship between employees of the organization and knowledge consultants, or between different knowledge consultants themselves. Without effective management, each may feel threatened by the other and consequently fail to cooperate in a way that best serves the company.

Similarly to the way that vested employees display stronger loyalty to the employer, weak affiliations between consultants and the enterprise may potentially lessen the benefits of the relationship. Expert consultants work with a variety of businesses and might be expected to display equal dedication to each one, however Barley and Kunda (2006) theorized that structured, legally reviewed contracts, work tracking documents, and periodic progress reviews may help keep the relationship on track. Aside from these precautions, the small business owner who uses appropriate communication strategies in consultancy relationships will benefit most. The sharing of organizational and personal goals and clear communication of intentions and expectations are critical. Finally, with regard to pricing structures, the business owner must regard the knowledge worker's skill, experience, and contribution potential when negotiating a fee structure. Engaging an expert, consulting firm, or contingent knowledge worker at an unusually discounted rate will fail to engender trust and dedication from the consultant (Barley & Kunda, 2006).

Owners and managers of small business enterprises have neither the time nor the resources to engage in all of the intense knowledge creation efforts required to move their organizations forward in today's competitive marketplace. Fortunately, the construct of the contingent workforce now embraces a variety of sophisticated services related to the creation of knowledge and the support of decision-making. Disadvantages of the knowledge consultancy relationship (versus internal employee resources) include a potential lack of continuity, a less-than-full-time dedication and availability of resources, limited control, and potentially higher cost. Despite these risks, the overarching benefits offered, including flexibility, potential overall and long-term cost savings, and, most significantly, the access provided to knowledge and expertise not previously available to the enterprise, combine to offset any potential drawbacks (Bannock, 2005).

The continued success and growth of small businesses are critical to the future economic health of the United States (Adla, Laskri, & Soubie, 2007). The potential benefits of various decision support systems are as significant for the small business enterprise as for its larger counterparts, provided the enterprise owner or decision-maker understands the adjustments required for a small company, and as long as the program and consultants are properly managed by the owner. The critical nature of the small business to American economic prosperity will best be served when the business community understands that the problems of small business are different from, but as significant as, those of their larger counterparts, and the theoretical approach to their management adapts accordingly.

Organizational Intelligence Policy

Concepts of Organizational Intelligence (OI) provide the enterprise with a wide variety of tools that, if managed properly, will allow the organization to grow and thrive through the creation of new knowledge. Current business pressures require the enterprise to be agile and innovative, while remaining grounded in sound industry practices. Information systems and technologies (IS/IT), when used in the proper context by the organization, provide both innovation and stability, and ensure that enterprise data, information, and knowledge are accurate, secure, and in compliance with industry and governmental regulation. A new Organizational Intelligence Policy is proposed herein for the Phoenix Insurance Company, addressing issues of data collection and security, queries and reporting, training, business unit structure, and strategic partnerships with constituents, users, and consultants.

The contemporary business climate places expectations on the enterprise to thrive while adapting to a rapidly changing set of rules and expectations. Despite the need to perform in an agile and innovative manner, companies must ground themselves with tools that lend stability and order. The sphere of information and knowledge systems technologies provides an invaluable opportunity to help the organization succeed; however this discipline may also expose the company to compromise. Lack of data governance, control, or security exposes the enterprise to instability, inaccuracy, or possibly even violation. To best leverage the opportunities offered by data and information management technology, the enterprise must adopt a comprehensive organizational intelligence policy.

Rod Kamal Ghani Agha, Ph.D.

Data Protection

Although many countries have adopted comprehensive and unified data protection laws, the United States government has thus far refused to do so. The U.S. prefers instead to let the private sector regulate itself and to address only limited aspects of data protection (Kayworth & Whitten, 2010). The federal government has enacted some legislation applicable to aspects of data security, and several states and municipalities have adopted more aggressive laws regarding this topic. Private sector executives and decision-makers must diligently adopt stewardship of data protection within their enterprise, and provide solid leadership for company technology personnel to follow. Data privacy, protection, and security are critical concepts to ensure the successful proliferation of electronic information storage technologies.

This almost incomprehensible volume of data that is accumulated, stored, and transmitted by U.S. companies has become an area of key concern for industry. Personal financial data, corporate intellectual property, and employee personal information must all be protected from external threats, while still remaining available to the enterprise as needed. The European Union convenes periodic conventions during which data protection guidelines are adopted. Member countries are given deadlines by which they must each enact legislation that complies with these guidelines (Data Privacy Day, 2011). Canada has enacted and regularly updates comprehensive legislation in the form of their Personal Information Protection and Electronic Documents Act, regulating data security for private industry (Data Privacy Day, 2011). The United States has adopted federal legislation pertaining to specific industries only, choosing to allow private enterprise to self-regulate most aspects of data protection and security. The U.S. Department of Commerce has published a "safe harbor arrangement" as a guideline for U.S. companies doing business with European companies so that domestic enterprise might comply with European data privacy regulations (United States Privacy Laws, 2011).

Many companies engage in data transmission using the Internet. The Internet poses a particularly weak point where data security may be compromised. The World Wide Web Consortium (W3C) has developed an overarching privacy protocol, the Platform for Privacy Preferences Project (P3P). P3P advocates encoding privacy and data management practices into websites and also allows individual data users to develop their own P3P profile (United States Data Privacy Laws, 2011). Various standards organizations such as the Organization for the Advancement of Structured Information Standards (OASIS) establish policy and make recommendations for a variety of electronic data issues. In 2009, the United States Senate and House of Representatives first voted unanimously to observe a National Day of Data Privacy to raise awareness of data security (Data Privacy Day, 2011).

Some specific legislation has been enacted in the United States, addressing issues of data security, data veracity, or privacy issues. Perhaps the most controversial and far-reaching is the federal Sarbanes-Oxley Act of 2002 (SOX), enacted in response to the failure and ultimate scandals of Enron, WorldCom, and others (Carroll & Buchholz, 2009). Sarbanes-Oxley is also known as the "Corporate and Auditing Accountability and Responsibility Act," and applies only to publically traded companies. SOX imposes an arduous set of accounting and reporting requirements on public firms, designed to protect the American public from misleading profitability representation and any subsequent financial damage that may result from depending on misrepresentation (Carroll & Buchholz, 2009). With specific regard to data policies and digital data security, SOX standardizes electronic data management systems and requires strict audit controls to ensure data and reporting accuracy.

The Federal Information Security Management Act of 2002 (FISMA) is a very comprehensive piece of legislation, designed to ensure information security within federal agencies. FIMSA considers information security a means to safeguard data and information systems from "unauthorized access use, disclosure, disruption, modification, or destruction in order to provide integrity, confidentiality and availability" (United States Privacy Laws, 2011). The standards and guidelines of FIMSA include a requirement that governmental agencies implement and maintain an inventory of significant information systems used by the agency. Further, the agency must rank data and data systems by risk level, depending on the type of data used. Minimum security controls must be implemented and risk assessments conducted. Security controls and system documentation must be monitored and must maintain reliability for the agency's FISMA accreditation to remain valid (United States Privacy Laws, 2011).

California, one state that often leads the country in progressive legislative actions, adopted SB 1836 in 2003. SB 1836, known as the Personal Information: Privacy Act, requires any state agency, business, or person conducting business in California to disclose any breach of security in which unencrypted personal information is obtained by unauthorized persons (United States Privacy Laws, 2011). Massachusetts enacted an even more comprehensive statute with 201 CMR 17.00, a set of regulations pertaining to Massachusetts General Law Chapter 93H. This legislation requires any entity that collects, uses, or stores the personal information of Massachusetts residents, either in analog form or electronically, adopt a written protection plan. This law also requires ongoing audits of the plan's efficacy (Commonwealth of Massachusetts, 2009).

Also of interest on the topic of data security, the federal Health Insurance Portability and Accountability Act (HIPPA) contains significant provisions of privacy and security, relating to the personal medical history data of Americans. The Security Rule provision of HIPPA addresses specifically the subject of electronically maintained protected health information (EPHI). The Security Rule requires that any entity that collects or maintains protected data adopt written policy standards for the protection of that information. In addition, the Security Rule establishes guideline requirements for training programs to ensure compliance and requires written contingency plans in the event of a security breach (United States Department of Health and Human Services, 2011).

Even without a comprehensive set of federally mandated oversight procedures, companies must understand the critical nature of self-regulating data security matters (Simons, 2009). Enterprise owners, executives, and key decision-makers might ideally seek out and embrace responsible data protection policies; however data technology specialists may encounter management resistance when attempting to design or implement comprehensive data governance policies. Core principles of stakeholder management dictate at minimum statutory compliance and the avoidance of any actions that may expose the enterprise to legal liability (Carroll & Buchholz, 2009). In the current technological climate, however, executives expose the enterprise to significant potential harm if all matters of data security are not taken seriously and acted upon.

The database designer can best achieve executive buy-in on issues of data protection by demonstrating how these measures will benefit the company and benefit the decision-makers (Rothman, 2008). Many executives do not have a detailed understanding of current technology and they may be fearful of it and consequently resistant to it. Of greater concern, executives may not understand the degree to which data compromise could negatively affect the enterprise and they may even believe that information technology staff overstate or overestimate the danger of threat (Rothman, 2008). What high level decision-makers do understand is the "bottom line" of corporate profitability.

Database designers and related information technology professionals must possess a comprehensive and up-to-date understanding of threats to data security. They can then demonstrate this understanding, using their own communications skills and understanding of management considerations, to convey to executives the importance of securing information and data stores. Communicating to executives on their terms, using the language of responsibility and decision-making, will allow the data management professional to convey the importance of data protection (Kayworth & Whitten, 2010).

Some topics that high level decision-makers will understand, and that data professionals may call on to help them achieve executive buy-in, are compliance, accountability, and cost containment. Most important, executives respond best to a balanced approach that calls on elements of corporate culture to successfully incorporate data security measures (Kayworth & Whitten, 2010). If executives perceive that critical security needs can be balanced with organizational goals and the culture of the company, chances for buy-in will be much greater. To achieve this goal, the data professional must grasp the importance of all critical business unit components and understand how the goals of each can be met while still maintaining the required level of enterprise data security.

Database professionals may employ a number of strategies to assist their firm in regulation and compliance. The first step is to develop and implement an effective approach to data governance. Sound data governance design requires a broad perspective reflective of enterprise goals, culture, and decision-making paradigms (Khatri & Brown, 2010). Enterprise accountability structures must also be considered in designing effective data governance, to clearly define who shall be responsible for decision-making and determining data standards. The significant benefit and purpose of establishing sound data governance policies early in the design process is that this policy will provide a reliable guideline against which all other data decisions may be accurately made.

Legislation may be imposed from a federal, state, or municipal level. If the enterprise conducts business abroad, those countries may also have legislative requirements. Some industry oversight organizations, such as those that are involved with the medical community, may have specific compliance requirements for those firms operating within their parameters. Each governing body that requires data compliance may issue regular updates or add requirements periodically (Smith, Winchester, Bunker, & Jamieson, 2010). As a part of data governance and formalized data management policies, technology professionals must establish ways to ensure the enterprise adheres to current requirements and plans for future changes in compliance obligations. Regular consultation with legal advisors familiar with compliance issues will further assist the enterprise in ensuring that all compliance requirements are met.

Kayworth and Whitten (2010) recommend a clear separation between those responsible for establishing security policy and those who enforce the policy. Those who perform significant data operations may also best be removed from policy making. In this way, those in charge over significant security decisions will not be distracted by operational considerations. Many operational "shortcuts" that could compromise data security can be avoided through the establishment of this separation.

Care must be taken to ensure that employees do not take steps to compromise enterprise data security (Siponen, Mahmood, & Pahnila, 2009). Ideally, hard-coded security restrictions will limit the damage that could result from employees' failure to comply with security policies, however areas of vulnerability will always be present in any situation. Key to avoiding this type of security breach is to ensure that all employees understand security policies and why they are necessary to the organization. A high degree of visibility to other associates and the resulting peer pressure has been shown to be effective at making employees comply with data security practices (Siponen, Mahmood, & Pahnila, 2009). Recruiting liaison advocates among both management and production staff to act as mediators may help convince workers of the importance of data security practices.

Self-policing practices and internal self-audits may be the most effective tool to help the enterprise comply with governing policies and requirements. External data audits may be an ongoing requirement for the enterprise, depending on its operational industry. If the enterprise is prepared for external audits however, the outcome is typically superior. Comprehensive self-audits will effectively prepare the organization for any external audit events (Simons, 2009).

A thorough understanding of external audit conditions and procedures will allow the enterprise to establish periodic self-audits, designed to monitor compliance with those requirements. Simons (2009) suggested that the enterprise may set up an effective self-audit program using the following steps. The enterprise must understand all requirements and procedures of the body that will perform the formal audit process. Clear and documented data management policies that specifically address potential items of concern for the external auditor will demonstrate the organization's commitment to compliance. Periodic internal audits that monitor data security systems, technologies, and practices should be documented and shared with the external auditor. Steps taken by the organization to correct security breaches or to better meet compliance requirements should be shared with external auditors, rather than held back. These proactive steps will demonstrate to auditing bodies the organization's commitment to compliance.

Securing data from attack should be the concern of every member of the enterprise. Because companies do not always maintain sufficient internal controls however, governmental restrictions are often implemented to ensure the safety of sensitive information. Ideally, these governing policies should be viewed as the minimum data security requirements by the enterprise. The application of multiple organizational approaches to data security policy, including the commitment of key management and information technology personnel to policy enforcement, will help assure successful enterprise compliance.

References

Amundson, S. D. (1998). Relationships between theory-driven empirical research in operations management and other disciplines. *Journal of Operations Management, 16,* 341-359.

Bacharach, S. B. (1989). Organizational theories: Some criteria for evaluation. *Academy of Management Review, 14*(4), 496-515. doi:10.5465/AMR.1989.4308374

Baskerville, R. L., & Myers, M. D. (2009). Fashion waves in information systems research and practice. *MIS Quarterly, 33*(4), 647-662.

Benbasat, I., & Weber, R. (1996). Research commentary: Rethinking "diversity" in information systems research. *Information Systems Research, 7*(4), 389-399.

Benbasat, I., & Zmud, R. W. (1999). Empirical research in information systems: The practice of relevance. *MIS Quarterly, 23*(1), 3-16.

Carlo, J. L., Lyytinen, K., & Rose, G. M. (2011). Internet computing as a disruptive information technology innovation: The role of strong order effects. *Journal of Information Systems, 21,* 91-122. doi:10.1111/j.1365-2575.2009.00345.x

Cavusoglu, H., Hu, N., Li, Y., & Ma, D. (2010). Information technology diffusion with influentials, imitators, and opponents. *Journal of Management Information Systems, 27*(2), 305-334.

Constantinides, P., Chiasson, M. W., & Introna, L. D. (2012). The ends of information systems research: A pragmatic framework. *MIS Quarterly, 36*(1), 1-20.

Ellis, T. & Levy, Y. (2008). Framework of problem-based research: A guide for novice researchers on the development of a research-worthy problem. *Informing Science: The International Journal of an Emerging Transdiscipline, 11,* 17-33.

Freese, L. (1980). Formal theorizing. *Annual Review of Sociology, 6*(1), 187.

Gelso, C. (2006). Applying theories to research: The interplay of theory and research in science. In Leong, F. T., & Austin, J. T. (Eds.), *The psychology research handbook*. Thousand Oaks, CA: Sage Publications.

Gregor, S. (2006). The nature of theory in information systems. *MIS Quarterly, 30*(3), 611-642.

Harlow, E. (2009). Contribution, theoretical. *Encyclopedia of Case Study Research.*

King, J., & Lyytinen, K. (2004). Reach and grasp. *MIS Quarterly, 28*(4), 539-551.

Kock, N. (2009). Information systems theorizing based on evolutionary psychology: An interdisciplinary review and theory integration framework. *MIS Quarterly, 33*(2), 395-412.

Larkins, A. G., & McKinney, C. W. (1980). Four types of theory: Implications for research in social education. *Theory & Research in Social Education, 8*(1), 9-17.

Lyytinen, K., & King, J. (2004). Nothing at the center?: Academic legitimacy in the information systems field 12. *Journal of the Association for Information Systems, 5*(6), 220-246.

Myers, M. D., & Klein, H. K. (2011). A set of principles for conducting critical research information systems. *MIS Quarterly, 35*(1), 17-36.

Rogers, E. M. (2003). *Diffusion of innovations.* (5th ed.). New York, NY: Free Press. ISBN: 978-0743222099

Scarbrough, H., & Swan, J. (2001). Explaining the diffusion of knowledge management: The role of fashion. *British Journal of Management, 12*(1), 3-13.

Siguaw, J. A., Simpson, P. M., & Enz, C. A. (2006). Conceptualizing innovation orientation: A framework for study and integration of innovation research. *Journal of Product Innovation Management, 23*, 556-574.

Stam, H. (2007). Theoretical psychology. *The International Handbook of Psychology*, SAGE Publications.

Stam, H. (2010). Theory. *Encyclopedia of Research Design,* SAGE Publications.

Wacker, J. (1998). A definition of theory: Research guidelines for different theory-building research methods in operations management. *Journal of Operations Management, 16*(4), 361–385.

Wagner, D. (2007). The limits of theoretical integration. *Social Justice Research, 20*(3), 270-287. doi:10.1007/s11211-007-0045-9

Wang, P. (2010). Chasing the hottest IT: Effects of information technology fashion on organizations. *MIS Quarterly, 34*(1), 63-85.

Weber, R. (1987). Toward a theory of artifacts: A paradigmatic base for information systems research. *Journal of Information Systems, 1*(2), 3.

Weber, R. (2003). Theoretically speaking. *MIS Quarterly, 27*(3), 331.

Weber, R. (2006). Reach and grasp in the debate over the IS core: An empty hand?. *Journal of the Association for Information Systems, 7*(10), 703-713.

Weber, R. (2012). Evaluating and developing theories in the information systems discipline. *Journal of the Association of Information Systems, 13*(1), 1-30.

Case Study V

Project Governance ERP Implementation Project

The implementation and application of enterprise resource planning architecture and systems is highly complex with many potentially critical implications for the enterprise, regardless of the organization's size. Every aspect of the project is highly interconnected and the challenges and problems inherent require a high degree of project governance, if the implementation is to be successful. Stakeholder constituents each have specific interests and those must be carefully identified and aligned with the strategic goals of the organization. The overall theoretical framework that results from this alignment may then be applied to the ERP architecture through the governance and change management processes. The result, when tempered with best practices and careful consideration of all critical risk and success factors, will provide the framework through which the enterprise may grow and thrive in a global economic environment.

Haines (2009) observed that, for the purpose of enterprise strategic alignment, the specialization of business assets must rightly link with the company's strategic goals. Enterprise resource management, particularly when customized for the organization, may be considered as exactly that type of specialization. Although best practices and logic might seem to dictate that companies would inherently align enterprise resource management with the organization's strategic goals, the relevant literature indicates that this critical link is frequently absent or not considered sufficiently to meet the company's needs. Project governance to incorporate business process modeling into the resource planning process will provide a reliable basis for implementation. In the case of Dencon Enterprises, Inc., project governance and a customized ERP system were the critical components of designing, planning, and implementing a successful enterprise resource architecture.

Background and Conceptual Framework

Indihar Stemberger, Bosilj Vuksic, and Kovacic (2009) defined the enterprise resource planning (ERP) system as an integrated approach to business management that consists of interrelated modules designed for systemically managing the processes and functions of an organization. The ERP system typically includes applications and tools that manipulate and integrate organizational data and information in ways that may allow the enterprise to create new knowledge or apply its existing knowledge in ways that improve the company's ability to compete in its market. Efficiency is improved, functions and processes are integrated, and the enterprise becomes operationally more effective within the framework of a successful ERP implementation (Sumner, 2009). Relevant literature has demonstrated that ERP systems are necessary in today's aggressive, globalized economy, if the company is to not only survive but thrive (Niehaves, Klose, & Becker, 2006).

Ghosh and Skibniewski (2010) evaluated risk factors and critical success factors of enterprise resource planning system implementation. Discussion of theory, although complex, provides a deceptively simple overview of what is actually a highly complex process. The evaluation of both risk and success factors, and the eventual mapping of each one, will provide a comprehensive guideline from which implementation may be guided. Ghosh and Skibniewski observed that each organization possesses a unique set of environmental complexities that govern its policies and processes. When considering these factors in the ERP design process, the organization must also consider cultural factors and the degree to which legacy systems and existing policies and processes are misaligned with the organization's goals, philosophies and culture. Implementation failures happen most frequently when the enterprise looks to the ERP architecture to emulate outdated or ineffective processes or those aspects of the business that are not currently aligned with critical strategic goals.

Niehaves, Klose, and Becker (2006) examined project governance as a critical component of ERP implementation, likening it to a complex political drama wherein the actors (directors, executives, managers, associates, and external stakeholders such as consultants and vendors) all negotiate to promote their own agendas and interests. Even those designated to coordinate project governance are likely to have interests they want served. Unless and until all stakeholders are in agreement about the strategic goals of the enterprise and how ERP will best serve those, the planning process must not begin.

Sumner (2009) explored relevant theory of alignment strategies for ERP implementation, noting that misalignment or bad "fit" often occurs upon introduction of ERP. The enterprise must often implement operational change that allows the organization and the ERP to reduce the gap. This gap may better be avoided and greater integration achieved between the organization's processes and goals through the utilization of ERPs that are specially designed to fit the organization's unique needs. Although predesigned ERP systems, known also as out-of-the-box solutions, may be adapted to the organization's individual needs, these work-arounds may result in major time delays and greater organizational challenges than would a truly customized ERP solution. Consequently, both approaches may be similar in both cost and time to implement (Sumner, 2009).

Case Study VI

Dencon Enterprises, Inc.

Dencon Enterprises, Inc. operates in the southwestern United States as a specialty developer and design-build contractor, serving the specific market of dental practice facility design and construction. This regional operation is a medium-sized business concern, with a home office located in Albuquerque, New Mexico, 12 regional offices throughout the Southwest, and approximately 250 employees. The company also regularly opens and closes on-site office facilities that operate for the duration of large projects. The company's business units include a land development and planning entity, an engineering and architectural entity, a construction enterprise, and a specialty interior finish and design entity.

In 2008, Dencon began the process of considering ERP implementation. Dencon had a variety of unique needs resulting from its innovative and diverse business practices. Unlike many traditional construction companies, Dencon provides an extended level of services that the client might normally have to obtain from a series of individual consultants and contractors. Using Dencon, the dental practice may identify and acquire a site for a new facility, design the building, have it built, and incorporate all the specialty dental equipment necessary for its operation, all from one integrated source. Dencon is unique not only because it provides this broad scale of services, but because it specializes in the dental practice field. Many companies perform aspects of what Dencon does, however few perform as many diverse services seamlessly.

Dencon's complex business model was rife with interdependent processes that were performed among and between distinct business units. As each business unit is its own independent operational entity (rather than simply a department within the company), Dencon's operations function more like that of a tightly networked virtual enterprise than a traditional stand-alone company. For accounting and audit purposes, each business unit must operate independently. For operational and project delivery purposes, the business units must function as one enterprise. Dencon's goal of implementing one cohesive ERP system for the enterprise appeared originally to be almost impossible, according to R.J. Voyette, the company's Chief Information Officer. Voyette explained that each unit was running a variety of legacy systems, almost none of which had interoperability with the others. Nevertheless, Dencon had performed process engineering for each business unit in advance of ERP implementation, and had determined that, except for the lack of interface capabilities, each unit's processes were highly effective and efficient.

Jeffrey Abbelouis, Dencon's Executive Vice President, Operations, was given the task of identifying a fully networked solution that would allow each unit to operate autonomously, network the processes of all units together seamlessly, support the home and regional offices, and allow on-site project offices to be put on- and off-line as necessary. Abbelouis and Voyette began the process of identifying an ERP solution that might meet those diverse needs. They quickly discovered that there were no packaged solutions available that truly met their needs.

Faced with the option of re-engineering a variety of business unit processes that were already efficient or customizing an ERP system for the company, Dencon's board of directors and key decision-makers elected to customize a system rather than disrupt enterprise operations. In 2008, Dencon's book for business through 2012 was over $480 million in long-term projects. Consequently, an effective and seamless ERP launch was critical, and disruptions had to be significantly minimized.

Mr. Voyette described Dencon's process for evaluation and vendor selection in great detail; however, the overarching theme to the process was that the company used a high level of discretion and best practices throughout the process. Dencon selected a solution provider, Aurigo, and choose Oracle + Masterworks as the basis for the enterprise resource network, from which each module was completely customized to emulate the legacy processes and systems and to provide the specific functionality the company required. The new system involved a high level of virtualization and software-as-a-service to reduce costs and provide for future scalability. Buy-in was obtained from every level of stakeholder, and the company's board of directors and executive management was supportive of the project from cradle to grave. Training began early and was conducted in a way that encouraged end-user input to develop the best possible level of cohesion.

Ultimately, Dencon's new ERP ran side by side with legacy systems for almost 30 days. Both management and users embraced the opportunity to view both systems together to detect any potential problems and to make adjustments to process control as necessary. At the end of the live test period, Aurigo launched one business unit at a time until the roll-out was complete. An aggressive change management policy was applied and a project team was installed to oversee ongoing project governance.

In the 30 months since the company took its new ERP system live, Mr. Voyette and Mr. Abbelouis listed several issues that have arisen with the system, however each has been addressed and handled in accordance with governance standards. The company has requested several changes to the system, however Aurigo also assigned a project team to work with Dencon on any changes or problems with the system. The two companies have an ongoing relationship that benefits both companies, at least from Dencon's perspective. Aurigo personnel did not contribute to this case study, however Voyette and Abbelouis expressed significant satisfaction with both Aurigo and the Oracle + Masterworks platform. The company declined to provide an overall cost of the project, however Voyette noted that, while the cost was high, the company had planned for the project for the three years prior to implementation. Both executives noted that the benefits of the ERP had been significant to the company and the return on investment was already being realized in a variety of ways.

Discussion

Dencon's case presents an exceptionally rare example of an almost flawless ERP implementation. Based on the relevant research and literature, Dencon employed a number of relevant best practices to the process. Haines (2009) observed that, when faced with the option of modifying business processes to mesh with ERP solutions, the enterprise must carefully consider the disruption that may result. The company may endeavor to modify its business processes, which is highly disruptive; the company may elect to implement the ERP system and leave its processes as they are, in which case significant process failure may occur; or the company may elect to customize an ERP solution to align with its processes. Haines observed that a lack of fit between systems and processes will inevitably lead to costly negative outcomes.

The fully integrated organization, as Dencon became through its ERP implementation, has increased efficiency and flexibility. Konsynski and Tiwana (2004) emphasized the importance of remaining adaptable and agile to compete in current global economic conditions. Dencon has retained its ability to adapt through both an aggressive change management program and an ongoing relationship with its solution provider, Aurigo. Inefficiencies have been diminished at Dencon, and complex intra- and interorganizational processes have been streamlined to allow the company to increase its production with a consistent level of staff. Konsynski and Tiwana stated that "a well-oiled extended enterprise is able to minimize transaction costs" (p. 235); Dencon has achieved this goal while also remaining agile and flexible.

Law, Chen, and Wu (2008) noted that companies have little guidance for ongoing ERP system maintenance, change management, user support, or ongoing requirements. Law et al further stated that, if the enterprise makes sound decisions on the front end of implementation, problems with the post-implementation issues may be significantly minimized. Choosing strong implementation partners, as Dencon appears to have done, is one critical consideration. Another factor that contributes to the minimization of back-end challenges involves the resolution of stakeholder conflict prior to implementation. Dencon Enterprises eliminated virtually all conflicts within the planning phase of the ERP project.

Sharma, Stone, and Ekinci (2009) noted that project governance, the most critical, overarching success factor of ERP system implementation, is based on three critical factors. Leadership provides clear objectives for decisions and leads strategic planning and policy. Scalable, flexible process improvement allows the organization to approach implementation without the burden of unwieldy absolutes, and provides an agile framework within which the enterprise evolves with the process rather than forcing the converse. Finally, the application of enabling technology for risk and problem resolution allows the enterprise to mitigate problems at every stage.

Taxonomy of Critical Considerations

Gattiker and Goodhue (2005) recommended that the enterprise pose several questions when first consideration a wide-scale ERP implementation project. The first and most important question is whether the implementation will produce a positive return on investment. If the organization is able to answer in the affirmative, the company must then seek to determine how this positive effect might be maximized. Next, the company must seek to identify all potential problems that may arise and how to minimize or eliminate those. Determining the ultimate effect on the enterprise may be difficult to truly determine, however these questions will provide a responsible initiation to the process.

Sumner (2009) stressed the critical nature of process evaluation and engineering, to ensure current enterprise processes align with the organization's strategic plans and goals. Customization of the ERP architecture serves to align enterprise processes with the solution environment, however if the organization's processes are not aligned correctly prior to the ERP project, flexibility and quality may never be achieved. Business process requirements include aspects of functional expertise, mechanisms for linking and liaison, scope, integration, and functional expertise. Sumner recommended the inclusion of "super users" (p. 434) throughout the process. These super users, typically far-removed from the planning, implementation, or management aspect of the ERP, instead have a unique perspective on the user process. Frequently, those responsible for implementation have little or no direct experience with the processes included and the addition of this perspective to the governance approach provides a real-world viewpoint to what is often a purely theoretical approach.

Čelar, Mudnić, and Gotovac (2011) described the importance of customization to effectively align sound enterprise processes with system functionalities. When contemplating ERP architecture, the company must first consider those ERP solutions that are available "out of the box," and evaluate how well each aligns with enterprise processes. Čelar et al further stated that the organization must perform a thorough cost benefit analysis to determine if it is better to change current enterprise processes to fit the boxed solution or to customize the application. Modifications to pre-packaged systems or even full-scale customizations, while generally regarded as more costly and time consuming than straightforward ERP adoptions, may actually take less time and cost less if appropriately managed.

Gefen (2004) emphasized the importance of establishing and maintaining a strong relationship of trust with ERP vendors and solution providers. Despite the application of best practices and careful governance, ERP system implementations inherently carry a significant risk and loss potential. Gefen further noted that, in ERP implementations involving a high level of customization, the risk potential increases significantly. Errors most often occur in the pre-implementation phase, when those errors are more difficult to detect. Trust evolves based on the perceived ability to predict the future behavior of another; identifying a vendor and solution provider who functions with integrity, ability, ethics, and high professional standards will assist the enterprise in developing a level of trust. Modeling these behaviors back to the implementation partners will further help establish a relationship of mutual trust.

Project governance, according to a large portion of the relevant research and literature, is one of the most important critical success factors for ERP implementation. Sharma, Stone, and Ekinci (2009) described governance as the process through which the enterprise ensures that a project, in this case ERP system installation, "is carried out property to achieve the desired results" (p. 30). Effective project governance establishes clear sponsorship and ownership of all aspects of the project, assigns and controls the use of resources for the project, applies to all direct (internal and external) stakeholders, and assigns direct and ongoing accountability for both project components and its overall, aggregate success.

Sharma, Stone, and Ekinci (2009) stated that change management is an extremely important element of a successful ERP implementation and ongoing improvement, wherein the enterprise may ensure that standardized methods and procedures are established to handle any required changes. Responsive and responsible change management practices are a part of project governance, however they are important enough to mention individually as a part of this taxonomy. Sumner (2009) noted that a critical component of change management is the development of new skill sets for both end users and implementers. Both training and re-skilling contribute significantly to project success, and must be considered as a critical component of the project governance taxonomy.

Conclusion

The implementation and application of enterprise resource planning architecture and systems is highly complex with many potentially critical implications for the enterprise, regardless of the organization's size. Every aspect of the project is highly interconnected and the challenges and problems inherent require a high degree of project governance, if the implementation is to be successful. Stakeholder constituents each have specific interests and those must be carefully identified and aligned with the strategic goals of the organization. The overall theoretical framework that results from this alignment may then be applied to the

ERP architecture through the governance process. The result, when tempered with best practices and careful consideration of all critical risk and success factors, will provide the framework through which the enterprise may grow and thrive.

Literature Review

The implementation process is critical to the overall success of ERP and much of the relevant literature has been dedicated to this topic. Indihar Stemberger, Bosilj Vuksic, and Kovacic (2009) described the importance of basing ERP systems on the modeled business processes of the enterprise. A variety of critical success and failure factors have been documented in ERP applications, however the key to a successful experience depends on the organization's critical examination of its own business processes. Its current processes may not best meet the company's goals and, if that's the case, basing the ERP around those existing practices will only take the company further away from a best practice environment. Tan, Steele, and Tolman (2009) also examined critical success factors in implementing ERP, noting the special importance of upper management support for the project's success. In addition, a comprehensive change management is necessary, as is maintaining a close relationship with those vendors and third-party consultants that are responsible for the technology transfer.

Ghosh and Skibniewski (2010) stressed the importance of viewing the ERP implementation process as systemic rather than liner, as is typically the case. Environmental complexities are rife within any enterprise, and different for each. Consequently, no true exemplar exists on which the organization should base its efforts; rather, each enterprise must examine its own complex environmental and political environment and apply those to implementation. Niehaves, Klose, and Becker (2006) supported this assertion, but emphasized the influence of political aspects of the organizational environment and the way each stakeholder's own interests may become incorporated into ERP implementation. Sumner (2009) proposed a variety of strategies that the enterprise might use to align its operational strategies, business goals, and the interests of direct stakeholders to achieve an ERP architecture that truly meshes with the enterprise's greatest needs. Sumner strongly recommended a high level of project governance to ensure a desired outcome.

Project governance has been a key theme in much of the relevant literature that addresses successful ERP implementation. Wilkin and Riddett (2009) examined managerial strategies for project governance, and the ways that these may constrain political influence and other self-centric influences that may jeopardize the success of ERP adoption. Sharma, Stone, and Ekinci (2009) discussed ERP project management and governance with Chief Executive Officers of several organizations that had recently undergone a major implementation. This study demonstrated an interesting variety of perspectives that emphasized the importance of experienced managers and established methodology in place for project governance. Even so, Sharma et al noted that project governance paradigms often need to be "shaken up" (p. 29) to re-articulate governance culture.

Gefen (2004) addressed the trust mechanisms necessary to achieve true usefulness in ERP implementation, emphasizing the criticality of trust as a success factor. Gefen asserted that trust was the most significant factor in determining the ultimate utility of the ERP system, especially as it relates to the implementation vendor. Gefen based this research on Zucker's theories of trust components, namely process-based trust, characteristic-based trust, and institution-based trust mechanisms. Both constituents in the relationship must feel that their business interaction is worthwhile and both must reliably meet their obligations to establish this trust, however the effort is ultimately worthwhile, according to Gefen, because the ultimate success of implementation will be significant.

Relative to the case study to be presented, Čelar, Mudnić, and Gotovac (2011) examined the customization of ERP, noting the significant amount of resources necessary. The complexity of customization is significant, especially for small- to medium-sized business enterprises; however, the scheduling component of project governance represents one significant aspect of a successful implementation of a custom ERP. Kumar and Keshan (2009) identified mapping of business processes as a critical aspect of governance that can deliver significant value. In addition, the inclusion of business rules provides a critical success factor for the incorporation of interdisciplinary project and system oversight. Implementation of ERP is critical for continuing system efficacy, however governance may not stop once implementation is achieved. Gattiker and Goodhue (2005) addressed issues of project governance once the system has "gone live" (p. 559). This issue is explored from the perspective of fit between organizational context and the specific processing mechanisms of the ERP. Law, Chen, and Wu (2010) also explored the full lifecycle of the ERP including maintenance and support, noting that post-implementation factors are equally important for system success. Konsynski and Tiwana (2004) addressed the implications of ERP implementation in a modern enterprise wherein the evolution of alliances and changing dynamics of networks defies the traditional paradigm of stability. Haines (2009) examined the factors that influence ERP customization when the enterprise is in pursuit of strategic alignment and dynamic networking opportunities. Key influences on customization must be examined as they relate to project governance, if the enterprise is to truly benefit from enterprise resource implementation.

References

Acgaoili, P. (2010). Disruptive technologies. Information Security, 12(8), 20-21.

Adla, A. A., Laskri, M. T., & Soubie, J. L. (2007). A cooperative framework for intelligent decision support systems. International Review on Computers & Software, 2(4), 292-301.

Ahmed, M., Chowdhury, A., Ahmed, M., & Rafee, M. (2012). An advanced survey on cloud computing and state-of-the-art research issues. International Journal of Computer Science Issues (IJCSI), 9(1-3), 201.

American Psychological Association (APA). (2010). Ethical principles of psychologists and code of conduct. Retrieved from http://www.apa.org/ethics/code/index.aspx

Amirkhani, A., Salehahmadi, Z., & Hajialiasgari, F. (2011). A new integrated TBT-TAM model for mobile marketing adoption in insurance sector. Interdisciplinary Journal of Contemporary Research in Business, 3(3), 855-866.

Amirkhani, A., Salehahmadi, Z., Kheiri, E., & Hajialiasgari, F. (2011). The TAM model's application in technology transition. Interdisciplinary Journal of Contemporary Research in Business, 3(3), 867-879.

Araz, C., & Ozkarahan, I. (2007). Supplier evaluation and management system for strategic sourcing based on a new multicriteria sorting procedure. International Journal of Production Economics, 106(2007), 585–606.

Assimakopoulos, N. A., Riggas, A. N. (2006). Designing a virtual enterprise architecture using structured system dynamics. Human Systems Management, 25(1), 13-29.

Avison, D. & Elliot, S. (2005), Scoping the discipline of information systems. In Avison, D. & Pries-Heje, J. (eds). Research in information systems: A handbook for research supervisors and their students, 3-18. Burlington, MA: Elsevier Butterworth-Heinemann. ISBN 0750666552.

Babey, E. (2006). Costs of enterprise resource planning system implementation—and then some. New Directions for Higher Education, (136), 21-33. doi:10.1002/he.237.

Backsourcing flexibility in IT services contracts. Journal of Management Information Systems, 26(4), 317-358.

Bagozzi, R. P., & Foxall, G. R. (1995). Construct validity and generalizability of the Kirton adaption-innovation inventory. European Journal of Personality, 9(3), 185-206.

Bannock, G. (2005). The economics and management of small business: An international perspective. New York, NY: Routledge.

Barley, S. R., & Kunda, G. (2006). Contracting: A new form of professional practice. Academy of Management Perspectives, 20(1), 45-66. doi:10.5465/AMP.2006.19873409.

Beckett, R. C. (2008). Utilizing and adaptation of the absorptive capacity concept in a virtual enterprise context. International Journal of Production Research, 46(5), 1243-1252. doi:10.1080/00207540701224327

Bell, E., & Bryman, A. (2007). The ethics of management research: An exploratory content analysis. British Journal of Management, 18(1), 63-77. doi:10.1111/j.1467-8551.2006.00487.x

Benaroch, M., Dai, Q., & Kauffman, R. J. (2010). Should we go our own way?

Berger, A. N. (2003). The economic effects of technological progress: Evidence from the banking sector. Journal of Money, Credit & Banking (Ohio State University Press), 35(2), 141-176.

Blackwell, P., Shehab, E. M., & Kay, J. M. (2006). An effective decision-support framework for implementing enterprise information systems within SMEs. International Journal of Production Research, 44(17), 3533-3552.

Booth, B., Laidlaw, R., Potts, C., Peppard, J., Rawlinson, R., Nagarajan, A., & Manwani, S. (2008). How do you make progress with an unpopular outsourced IT helpdesk. Computer Weekly, 14.

Bostrom, R. P., & Heinen, J. (1977). MIS problems and failures: A socio-technical perspective, Part II: The application of socio-technical theory. MIS Quarterly, 1(4), 11-28.

Bostrom, R. P., Gupta, S., & Thomas, D. (2009). A meta-theory for understanding information systems within sociotechnical systems. Journal of Management Information Systems, 26(1), 17-47.

Bradley, L., & Stewart, K. (2003). The diffusion of online banking. Journal of Marketing Management, 19(9/10), 1087-1109.

Bullock, M., & Panicker, S. (2003). Ethics for all: Differences across scientific society codes. Science & Engineering Ethics, 9(2), 159-170. Retrieved from http://www.springer.com /social+sciences/ applied+ethics/journal/11948

Cai, M. M., Zhang, W. Y., Chen, G. G., Zhang, K. K., & Li, S. T. (2010). SWMRD: a semantic web-based manufacturing resource discovery system for cross-enterprise collaboration. International Journal of Production Research, 48(12), 3445-3460. doi:10.1080/00207540902814330

Carlo, J. L., Lyytinen, K., & Rose, G. M. (2011). Internet computing as a disruptive information technology innovation: The role of strong order effects. Information Systems Journal, 21(1), 91-122. doi:10.1111/j.1365-2575.2009.00345.x.

Chao, C., & Chandra, A. (2012). Impact of owners' knowledge of information technology (IT) on strategic alignment and IT adoption in US small firms. Journal of Small Business and Enterprise Development, 19(1), 114-131. doi:10.1108/14626001211196433

Chen, T. Y., Chen, Y. M., Chu, H. C., & Wang, C. B. (2008). Distributed access control architecture and model for supporting collaboration and concurrency in dynamic virtual enterprises. International Journal of Computer Integrated Manufacturing, 21 (3), 301-324.

Chen, T. Y., Chen, Y. M., Chu, H. C., & Wang, C. B. (2008). Distributed access control architecture and model for supporting collaboration and concurrency in dynamic virtual enterprises. International Journal of Computer Integrated Manufacturing, 21(3), 301-324.

Chien-Hung, C., & Mort, G. (2007). Consumers' technology adoption behaviour: an alternative model. Marketing Review, 7(4), 355-368. doi:10.1362/146934707X251119.

Chin, W. W., Johnson, N., & Schwarz, A. (2008). A fast form approach to measuring technology acceptance and other constructs. MIS Quarterly, 32(4), 687-703.

Chong, A., Ooi, K. B., Tak, Y. K., & Yang, Z. S. (2009). Factors affecting the adoption of e-commerce: A study of the textile sector in Wujin, China. International Journal of Business & Management Science, 2(2), 117-130.

Chung, B.Y., Skibniewski, M., Kwak, Y.H. (2009). Developing ERP systems success model for the construction industry. Journal of Construction Engineering and Management, 135(3), 207.

Clark, T. D., Jones, M. C., & Armstrong, C. P. (2007). The dynamic structure of management support systems: Theory development: Research focus, and direction. MIS Quarterly, 31(3), 579-615.

Constantinides, P., Chiasson, M. W., & Introna, L. D. (2012). The ends of information systems research: A pragmatic framework. MIS Quarterly, 36(1), 1-20.

Davis, F. D. (1989). Perceived usefulness, perceived ease of use, and user acceptance of information technology. MIS Quarterly, 13(3), 319-340.

Desouza, K. C., & Awazu, Y. (2006). Contingent knowledge workers [contingent workers employment]. Engineering Management, 16(4), 18-19. doi:10.1049/em:20060402.

DeWitt, J. W. (2012). Cyber risk in 2012: Get your head in the cloud. National Underwriter/P&C, 116(9), 18-19.

Dlodlo, N. (2011). Legal, privacy, security, access and regulatory issues in cloud computing. Proceedings of the European Conference on Information Management & Evaluation, 161-168.

Dowlatshahi, S. (2005). Strategic success factors in enterprise resource-planning design and implementation: a case-study approach. International Journal of Production Research, 43(18), 3745-3771. doi:10.1080/00207540500140864.

Doyle, E., Mullins, M., & Cunningham, M. (2010). Research ethics in a business school context: The establishment of a review committee and the primary issues of concern. Journal of Academic Ethics, 8(1), 43-66. doi:10.1007/s10805-010-9108-x

Dragoi, G., Rosu, L., Rosu, S., & Radovici, A. (2009). Virtual enterprise network solutions for virtual product development in the Preminv e-platform. Annals of DAAAM & Proceedings, 165-166.

Duan, Y. & Xu, M. (2005). Decision support systems in small business. University of Louton and Portsmouth, UK, Encyclopedia of Information Science and Technology, 754-758

Dwivedi, D. (2007). ERP software for small business. Chemical Business, 21(6), 27.

Ehmke, C., Akridge, J., Lusk, C., & Lusk, J. (2004, July). Selecting and managing consultants. New Ventures, Purdue University Agricultural Innovation and Commercialization Center, 719, 1-4.

Engineering News-Record, 264(10), 26.

Fest, G. (2011). Baby steps into the cloud. U.S. Banker, 121(3), 30.

Fichman, R. G. (2004). Going beyond the dominant paradigm for information technology innovation research: Emerging concepts and methods. Journal of the Association for Information Systems, 5(8), 314-355.

Ford, N.J. (2006). The development and evaluation of an information technology support system to facilitate inter-organisational collaboration in HRD. Journal of European Industrial Training, 30(7), 569-588.

Frechtling, D., & Boo, S. (2012). On the ethics of management research: An exploratory investigation. Journal of Business Ethics, 106(2), 149-160. doi:10.1007/s10551-011-0986-7

Gill, G., & Bhattacherjee, A. (2009). Whom are we informing? Issues and recommendations for MIS research from an informing sciences perspective. MIS Quarterly, 33(2), 217-235.

Goo, J., & Huang, C. D. (2008). Facilitating relational governance through service level agreements in IT outsourcing: An application of the commitment–trust theory. Decision Support Systems, 46 (1), 216-232. http://dx.doi.org.proxy1.ncu.edu/10.1016 /j.dss.2008.06.005

Goo, J., Kishore, R., Rao, H. R., & Nam, K. (2009). The role of service level agreements in relational management of information technology outsourcing: An empirical study. MIS Quarterly, 33(1), 119-145.

Grant, I. (2007). Housing authority reaps efficiency gains from IT helpdesk application. Computer Weekly, 58.

Grant, K. (2010). Knowledge management, an enduring fashion. Proceedings of the International Conference on Intellectual Capital, Knowledge Management & Organizational Learning, 2010, 207-220.

Greaney, A., Sheehy, A., Heffernan, C., Murphy, J., Mhaolrunaigh, S., Heffernan, E., & Brown, G. (2012). Research ethics application: A guide for the novice researcher. British Journal of Nursing (BJN), 21(1), 38-43.

Gregor, S. (2006). The nature of theory in information systems. MIS Quarterly, 30(3), 611-642.

Hall, D. J., & Paradice, D. (2005). Philosophical foundations for a learning-oriented knowledge management system for decision support. Decision Support Systems, 39(2005), 445-461.

Hansson, S. (2011). Do we need a special ethics for research?. Science and Engineering Ethics, 17(1), 21-29.

Harris, C. (2011). Touching the cloud. Canadian Underwriter, 78(6), 32-40.

Hold, D., & Baltaxe, D. (2007). Enterprise end users moving to next-generation networks. Business Communications Review, 37(5), 28-34.

Horner, J., & Minifie, F. D. (2011). Research ethics: Publication practices and authorship, conflicts of interest, and research misconduct. Journal of Speech, Language & Hearing Research, 54(1), 346-362. doi:10.1044/1092-4388(2010/09-0263)

Howard, P. N., Anderson, K., Busch, L., & Nafus, D. (2009). Sizing up information societies: toward a better metric for the cultures of ICT adoption. Information Society, 25(3), 208-219. doi:10.1080/01972240902848948.

Hsiao, C.H., & Yang, C. (2011). The intellectual development of the technology acceptance model: A co-citation analysis. International Journal of Information Management, 31, 128-136. doi:10.1016/j.ijinfomgt.2010.07.003

Hua, G., Fei, T., Lin, Z., Suiyi, S., & Nan, S. (2010). Correlation-aware web services composition and QoS computation model in virtual enterprise. International Journal of Advanced Manufacturing Technology, 51(5-8), 817-827. doi:10.1007/s00170-010-2648-9

Huang, L., Quaddus, M., Rowe, A. L., & Lai, C. (2011). An investigation into the factors affecting knowledge management adoption and practice in the life insurance business. Knowledge Management Research & Practice, 9(1), 58-72. doi:10.1057/kmrp.2011.2

ISBN: 978-0743222099

Jaeger, J. (2011).Cloud computing poses new risks, opportunities. Compliance Week 86(8), 1.

Jagdev, H., Vasiliu, L., Browne, J., & Zaremba, M. (2008). A semantic web service environment for B2B and B2C auction applications within extended and virtual enterprises. Computers in Industry, 59(8), 786-797. Retrieved from

Janssens, G., Kusters, R., Heemstra, F. (2008). Sizing ERP implementation projects: an activity-based approach. International Journal of Enterprise Information Systems, 4(3), 25.

Jorgensen, E. R. (2005). Four philosophical models of the relationship between theory and practice. Philosophy of Music Education Review, 13(1), 21-36.

Karadag, E. (2011). Instruments used in doctoral dissertations in educational sciences in Turkey: Quality of research and analytical errors. Educational Sciences: Theory and Practice, 11(1), 330-334.

Kauffman, R. J., & Tsai, J. Y. (2009). The Unified Procurement Strategy for Enterprise Software: A Test of the "Move to the Middle" Hypothesis. Journal of Management Information Systems, 26(2), 177-204.

Kenealy, B. (2011). The disappearing data center. Insurance Networking News, 14(1), 14-18.

Kerimoglu, O., Basoglu, N., & Daim, T. (2008). Organizational adoption of information technologies: Case of enterprise resource planning systems. Journal of High Technology Management Research, 19, 21-35.

Kesner, R.M. (2010). The evolving symbiosis between decision support and knowledge management systems: A study in emerging industry practices. Journal of Knowledge Globalization, 3(2), 1-27.

Kim, C. C., Son, Y. J., Kim, T. T., & Kim, K. K. (2008). A virtual enterprise design method based on business process simulation. International Journal of Computer Integrated Manufacturing, 21(7), 857-868. doi:10.1080/09511920701813133

Krigsman, M. (2010, November). Understanding Lumber Liquidators' ERP failure. IT Project Failures, CNET.

Landsman, V., & Givon, M. (2010). The diffusion of a new service: Combining service consideration and brand choice. Quantitative Marketing & Economics, 8(1), 91-121. doi:10.1007/s11129-009-9077-9

Larsen, T. J. (2009). A multilevel explanation of end-user computing satisfaction with an enterprise resource planning system within an international manufacturing organization. Computers in Sector, 60 (9), 657-668. http://dx.doir.org.proxy1.ncu.edu /10.1016/j.compind.2009.05.004

Legris, P., Ingham, J., & Collerette, P. (2003). Why do people use information technology? A critical review of the technology acceptance model. Information & Management, 40,191-204. doi:10.1016/S0378-7206(01)00143-4

Lei, S. (2009). Research collaboration and publication during graduate studies: Evaluating benefits and costs from students' perspectives. College Student Journal, 43(4), 1163.

Liang, F. F., Fung, R. K., Jiang, Z. Z., & Wong, T. N. (2008). A hybrid control architecture and coordination mechanism in virtual manufacturing enterprise. International Journal of Production Research, 46(13), 3641-3663. doi:10.1080/00207540601100916

Liang, F. F., Fung, R. K., Jiang, Z. Z., & Wong, T. N. (2008). A hybrid control architecture and coordination mechanism in virtual manufacturing enterprise. International Journal of Production Research, 46(13), 3641-3663. doi:10.1080/00207540601100916

Liang, H., Nilesh, S., Hu, Q., & Xue, Y. (2007). Assimilation of enterprise systems: The effect of institutional pressures and the mediating role of top management. MIS Quarterly, 31(1), 59-87.

Lin, C., Shih, H., & Sher, P. J. (2007). Integrating technology readiness into technology acceptance: The TRAM model. Psychology & Marketing, 24(7), 641-657.

Low, C., Chen, Y., & Wu, M. (2011). Understanding the determinants of cloud computing adoption. Industrial Management + Data Systems, 111(7), 1006-1023. doi:10.1108/02635571111161262

McAfee, A. (2011). What every CEO needs to know about the cloud. Harvard Business Review, 89(11), 124-132.

Melville, N., & Ramirez, R. (2008). Information technology innovation diffusion: an information requirements paradigm. Information Systems Journal, 18(3), 247-273. doi:10.1111/j.1365-2575.2007.00260.x.

Miller, K. D., & Tsang, E. K. (2011). Testing management theories: Critical realist philosophy and research methods. Strategic Management Journal, 32(2), 139-158. doi:10.1002/smj.868.55532313

Moore, G. C., & Benbasat, I. (1991). Development of an instrument to measure the perceptions of adopting an information technology innovation. Information Systems Research, 2(3), 192-222.

Moore, G. C., & Benbasat, I. (1991). Development of an instrument to measure the perceptions of adopting an information technology innovation. Information Systems Research, 2(3), 192-222.

Natarajan, C. R. (2008). Deception and informed consent in management research. ICFAI Journal of Management Research, 7(1), 7-36.

National Academy of Sciences (NAS). (2009). On being a scientist: A guide to responsible conduct in research. (3rd ed.). Washington, D.C.: National Academies Press.

NetSuite. (2010). Run all key back-office operations with a single web-based financials/ ERP application. NetSuite Financials.

O'Leary, D. (2008). Supporting decisions in real-time enterprises: Autonomic supply chain systems. Information Systems and eBusiness Management, 6(3), 239-255.

Orbach, Y., & Fruchter, G. E. (2010). A utility-based diffusion model applied to the digital camera case. Review of Marketing Science, 8(1), 1-26.

Pan, M. J., & Jang, W. Y. (2008). Determinants of the adoption of enterprise resource planning within the technology-organization-environment framework: Taiwan's communications sector. Journal of Computer Information Systems, 48(3), 94-102.

Pearson. (2011). Executive concepts in business strategy. Pearson Learning Solutions. ISBN: 9780558870638.

Power, D. J. (2002). Decision support systems: Concepts and resources for managers. Westport, Conn., Quorum Books.

Prajapati, B., Dunne, M., & Armstrong, R. (2010). Sample size estimation and statistical power analyses. Optometry Today, 50(20), 1-9.

Puelz, R. (2010). Technology's effect on property–casualty insurance operations. Risk Management & Insurance Review, 13(1), 85-109. doi:10.1111/j.1540-6296.2009.01175.x

Reed, J. H., & Jordan, G. (2007). Using systems theory and logic models to define integrated outcomes and performance measures in multi-program settings. Research Evaluation, 16(3), 169-181. doi:10.3152/095820207X243909

Riaz Ahamed, S. S., & Rajamohan, P. P. (2011). Comprehensive performance analysis and special issues of virtual private network strategies in the computer communication: A novel study. International Journal of Engineering Science & Technology, 3(7), 6040-6048.

Richardson, J. (2009). Diffusion of technology adoption in Cambodia: The test of a theory. International Journal of Education & Development Using Information & Communication Technology, 5(3), 1-15.

Rogers, E. M. (2003). Diffusion of innovations. (5th ed.). New York: Free Press. ISBN: 978-0743222099

Ruquet, M. E. (2011). Cloud computing popularity growing, but what's the risk for agencies? National Underwriter, 115(40), 18.

Ryan, M. D. (2011). Cloud computing privacy concerns on our doorstep. Communications of The ACM, 54(1), 36-38. doi:10.1145/1866739.1866751

Salles, M. (2006). Decision making in SMEs and information requirements for competitive intelligence. Production Planning & Control, 17(3), 229-237.

Savage, G., Bunn, M., Gray, B., Xiao, Q., Wang, S., Wilson, E., & Williams, E. (2010). Stakeholder collaboration: Implications for stakeholder theory and practice. Journal of Business Ethics, 9621-26. doi:10.1007/s10551-011-0939-1

Sawyer, T. (2010). Enterprise resource planning systems break down data silos. ENR:

Sein, M. K., Henfridsson, O., Purao, S., Rossi, M., & Lindgren, R. (2011). Action design research. MIS Quarterly, 35(1), 37-56.

Sen, S., Raghu, T. S., & Vinze, A. (2010). Demand information sharing in heterogeneous IT services environments. Journal of Management Information Systems, 26(4), 287-316.

Sethi, Vij., Sethi, Vik., Jeyaraj, A., & Duffy, K. (2008). Enterprise resource planning systems implementation in a global subsidiary organization: Lessons learned. Journal of Asia - Pacific Business, 9(4), 373.

Setia, P., Setia, M., Krishnan, R., & Sambamurthy, V. (2011). The effects of the assimilation and use of IT applications on financial performance in healthcare organizations. Journal of the Association for Information Systems, 12(3), 274-298.

Smith, R. (2009). Computing in the cloud. Research Technology Management, 52(5), 65-68.

Sugang, M. (2012). A review on cloud computing development. Journal of Networks, 7(2), 305-310. doi:10.4304/jnw.7.2.305-310

Taylor, H., Dillon, S., & Van Wingen, M. (2010). Focus and diversity in information systems research: Meeting the dual demands of a healthy applied discipline. MIS Quarterly, 34(4), 647-667.

Thomson, R. (2007). Management software boosts IT helpdesk efficiency at NHS trust. Computer Weekly, 43.

Vaccaro, V. L., Ahlawat, S., & Cohn, D. Y. (2010). Diffusion of innovation, marketing strategies, and global consumer values for a high technology product. International Journal of Business Strategy, 10(3), 113-128.

Venkatesh, V., & Bala, H. (2008). Technology acceptance model 3 and a research agenda on interventions. Decision Sciences, 39(2), 273-315. doi:10.1111/j.1540-5915.2008.00192.x.

Wang, W. Y. C., Rashid, A., & Chuang, H. M. (2011). Toward the trend of cloud computing. Journal of Electronic Commerce Research, 12(4), 238-242.

Watson, H. (2009). Disruptive and Sustaining Technologies in BI Software. Business Intelligence Journal, 14(4), 4-6.

Weber, R. (2012). Evaluating and developing theories in the information systems discipline. Journal of the Association of Information Systems, 13(1), 1-30.

Westra, A. E., & de Beaufort, I. D. (2011). The merits of procedure-level risk-benefit assessment. IRB: Ethics & Human Research, 33(5), 7-13.

White, C. (2011). Data communications and computer networks: A business user's approach. Boston, MA: Cengage Press. ISBN 0538452617.

Xue, Y., Liang, H., Boulton, W. R., & Snyder, C. A. (2005). ERP implementation failures in China: Case studies with implications for ERP vendors. International Journal of Production Economics, 97 (3), 279-295. http://dx.doi.org.proxy1.ncu.edu/ 10.1016/j.ijpe.2004.07.008

Younghwan, C., Dongwoo, K., Heekwon, C., & Kwangsoo, K. (2008). An enterprise architecture framework for collaboration of virtual enterprise chains. International Journal of Advanced Manufacturing Technology, 35(11/12), 1065-1078. doi:10.1007/s00170-006-0789-7

Zadorozhny, V., Raschid, L., & Gal, A. (2008). Scalable catalog infrastructure for managing access costs and source selection in wide area networks. International Journal of Cooperative Information Systems, 17(1), 77-109.

Zamani, A., Akhtar, M., & Ahmad, S. (2011). Emerging cloud computing paradigm. International Journal of Computer Science Issues (IJCSI), 8(4), 304.

Relevant Terms

American Institute of Architects (AIA): United States professional association for architects; developer and sanctioning body for many construction documentation practices.

Building Information Management: supports the standards and requirements of data for use in Building Information Modeling projects.

Building Information Modeling (BIM): Defined workflows and modeling methods used to achieve specific, repeatable, and reliable information results; three-dimensional virtual modeling environment for construction design and coordination.

Building Product Model (BPM): data model detailing materials and specific construction methods to be incorporated into the construction project.

Computer-Aided Design/Drafting (CAD): electronic geometric design environment, primarily used by architects, engineers, and construction enterprises to design construction project documents; first-generation replacement for hand drafting.

Construction Documents: building plans, specifications, design guides, technical summaries, engineering calculations, contracts, and other related documentation that comprise the full, official scope of a building project.

Construction Operations Building Information Exchange (COBIE): formalized process protocol for the official transfer of construction documents from contractor to owner to include equipment lists, trade contractor warranties, maintenance schedules, and spare parts.

Construction Phase Cost Management: proactive and anticipatory process for planning and controlling project costs.

Construction Schedule: (also known as Construction Progress Documentation) time-scaled progress chart detailing each phase and task required for project completion, indicating planned start and end dates, to-date progress, and anticipated completion date; typical Construction Schedule may be represented as a Critical Path Method (CPM) schedule, Gantt chart, or PERT chart.

Construction Specifications Institute (CSI): organization that develops and maintains standardized construction language for use in building specifications.

Critical Path Method (CPM) Schedule: mathematically based algorithm used to schedule and track the progress of a project; project schedule modeling tool.

Earned Value Analysis: industry-standard method of measuring a project's progress at any given time, forecasting its completion date and final cost, and analyzing variances in the schedule and budget as the project proceeds.

Facility Condition Index (FCI): benchmark scale used to compare the relative condition of facilities or of one particular facility over time; used in asset management, often for public projects.

Gantt Chart: bar chart used to illustrate construction schedule; demonstrates start and finish dates and relational dependency of tasks.

Internal Collaborative Planning: project preparation that emphasizes individual team member strengths and team synergy; produces quantifiable business benefits that directly support the achievement of key project objectives such as cost or time savings.

Integrated Project Delivery (IPD): leverages early contributions of knowledge and expertise through the utilization of new technologies, allowing Project Team members to expand the value they provide throughout the project lifecycle.

Lean Project Delivery (LPD): project-based production process designed to manage and improve all dimensions of the built and natural environment using minimum cost and maximized value while meeting customer needs and limiting environmental impact.

Life Cycle Cost Analysis (LCCA): method for assessing the total cost of facility ownership; takes into account all costs of acquiring, owning, and disposing of a building or building system.

Program Evaluation and Review Technique (PERT) Chart: illustrative project management model used to represent task breakdown of a project.

Project Delivery Method: system used for planning, organizing, and facilitating design, construction, operations, and maintenance services for a structure or facility by entering legal agreements with one or more entities or parties.

Project Delivery Team: those professionals involved in the programming, planning, construction, and sub-contractor roles for the project.

Project Design Team: those professionals involved in the design, engineering, and permitting phase of the project; also involved with any structural modifications required during the construction phase.

Project Development Lifecycle: (also known as Systems Development Lifecycle) the process of creating or altering systems for the purpose of executing a specific project, and the models and methods used to develop these systems; standard divisions include planning, analysis, design, implementation, and maintenance.

Project Deployment Plan: defines and establishes the management strategy for achieving the goals of the project; purposes include guiding project execution, documenting project planning assumptions, documenting alternative project planning decisions, facilitating communication among team members, providing a baseline for progress measurement and project control.

Return on Investment (ROI): the ratio of money gained or lost on an investment relative to the money invested.

Sustainable Design: the practice of designing buildings and other objects to comply with the principles of social, economic, and ecological sustainability.

System Development Lifecycle: the process of creating, altering, planning, and controlling computer or information systems and the methods and models used in the development of these systems.

TAM: Technology Acceptance Model

Value Engineering: conscious and explicit set of disciplined procedures designed to seek out optimum value for both initial and long-term investment in a construction project.

Virtual Collaborative Building (VCB): integrated approach to design and construction utilizing virtual design and construction technologies wherein team members abandon traditional roles and apply new paradigms to workflows and communication efforts; using BIM technology, team members may frequently be located around the globe.

Virtual Design and Construction (VDC): the use of integrated multidisciplinary performance models of design-construction projects, including the product (facilities), work processes, and organization of the design – construction – operation team in order to support explicit and public business objectives.

U.S. National Institute of Standards and Technology (NIST): division of the U.S. Department of Commerce responsible for establishing construction technical guidelines and documentation.

www.ingramcontent.com/pod-product-compliance
Lightning Source LLC
LaVergne TN
LVHW042134040326
832903LV00001B/4